Leader's Guide

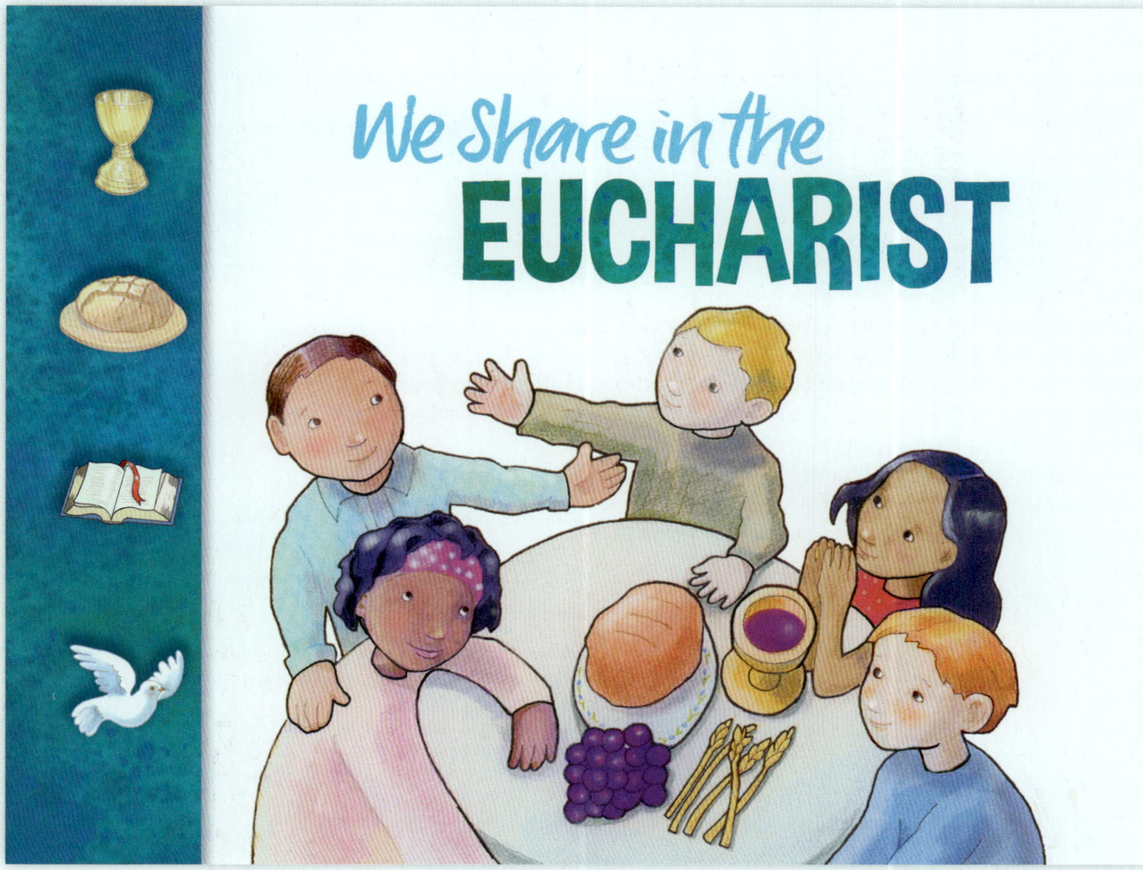

Authors
Françoise Darcy-Berube and Jean-Paul Berube

Editors
Gwen Costello and Myrtle Power

Sacramental Preparation Resources, 3rd edition
We Prepare for Reconciliation
We Share in the Eucharist

TWENTY-THIRD PUBLICATIONS

NOVALIS

Nihil Obstat
Caroline Altpeter IBVM
Archdiocese of Toronto
19 June 2009

Imprimatur
+Thomas Collins
Archbishop of Toronto
1 July 2009

Cover: Design: Celeste Gagnon; illustration: Anna Payne-Krzyzanowski

Design & Layout: Celeste Gagnon

Illustrations: ArtPlus: pp. 4, 25, 36; June Bradford: pp. 16, 18, 29, 34, 35, 37, 38, 45, 52, 56 and Prayer Book art; Heather Collins: pp. 15, 28, 30, 35, 42, 43, 48, 49; Vesna Krstanovic: p.13; Suzanne Mogensen: pp. 12, 36, 40, 46; Anna Payne-Krzyzanowski: pp. cover, 7, 8, 19, 20-24, 26, 27, 31, 39, 41, 51, 53, and icons.

Photo credits: Page 3: © WP Wittman Photography; Page 6: © iStockphoto.com/Legacy OnePhotography; Page 9: © WP Wittman Photography; Page 14: © WP Wittman Photography; Page 16: © WP Wittman Photography; Page 25: © WP Wittman Photography; Page 26: © WP Wittman Photography; Page 31: top left: © WP Wittman Photography; Page 31: bottom right: © WP Wittman Photography; Page 32: © WP Wittman Photography; Page 33: ?; Page 44: © WP Wittman Photography; Page 50: top right: © WP Wittman Photography; Page 50: bottom left: © WP Wittman Photography; Page 53: top left: © Juriah Mosin/Shutterstock; Page 53: bottom right: © iStockphoto.com/peanut8481; Page 54: © WP Wittman Photography

Publishing Office:
1 Eglinton Avenue East, Suite 800
Toronto, ON, Canada
M4P 3A1

Head Office:
4475 Frontenac Street
Montreal, QC, Canada
H2H 2S2

Tel: 416-363-3303 — Toll-Free: 1-877-702-7773
Fax: 416-363-9409 — Toll-Free: 1-877-702-7775
E-mail: resources@novalis.ca
www.novalis.ca
ISBN: 978-2-89688-672-2 (Novalis)

Cataloguing in Publication is available from Library and Archives Canada.

We acknowledge the support of the Government of Canada.

Published in the United States by
Twenty-Third Publications
A division of Bayard, Inc.
One Montauk Avenue, Suite 200
New London, CT 06320
www.twentythirdpublications.com

ISBN: 978-1-62785-457-3 (Twenty-Third Publications)
Library of Congress Control Number: 2019936391

Printed in Canada

Order extra activities for children free of charge at twentythirdpublications.com in the FREE E-Resources section.

Table of Contents

Welcome!

You are about to begin the journey of walking with parish children and their parents towards the sacrament of First Eucharist (or First Communion).

In the early Church, most people who sought to become Christians were adults. They were baptized and confirmed before celebrating the Eucharist. Over the years, influenced by both theology and practice, these three sacraments were separated. Children were baptized as infants; later, usually at age seven, they were prepared for Reconciliation before celebrating First Communion. Church leaders still require that children at least learn about sin and Reconciliation before First Communion; in some parishes, children celebrate the sacrament of Reconciliation when they are older.

This book focuses on First Eucharist, of course, but it also introduces children to a Christian way of life and prayer. It emphasizes the central place of Jesus as he is experienced at Sunday liturgy and invites children to become intimately acquainted with Jesus and with the Mass itself. It also emphasizes the concepts of thanksgiving, forgiveness, praise, remembering, and sacrifice, which pave the way for the sacrament. The final theme offers immediate preparation for First Communion.

We believe that you as a parish catechist, working with and walking with parents and their children, are immensely important as a guide and mentor in preparing children for their first experience of Eucharist. Enjoy the journey, and as you walk it, may you too experience a renewed devotion to the Eucharistic liturgy and to Jesus himself.

The Journey of Initiation

In this resource, the term "sacramental preparation" refers to preparing for the sacraments of initiation (Baptism, Eucharist, and Confirmation), and also, in conjunction with them, the sacrament of Reconciliation. This term does express what people are attempting to do before they celebrate these sacraments for the first time, but it doesn't take into account the *ongoing process* of entering into the mystery of Christ, which is discovered and experienced in the sacraments. This process is called Christian initiation. We slowly and continuously grow "into" Christ throughout our lifetimes. As we have already seen, the notion of initiation developed early on in the Church. This process for individuals and families took place in five clearly defined stages:

1. It had a precise beginning when the candidate's request to become a Christian was officially accepted.
2. The initiatory process began. During this stage, the candidate was taught how to live gospel values, learned about the Church's customs and traditions, and practised various forms of prayer.
3. When they were ready, the candidates celebrated Baptism and Confirmation, followed by participation in the Eucharistic meal.
4. The mystagogy period came next. At this time, the new Christian tried to deepen his or her experience of Christ by reflecting on all that had happened. (*Mystagogy* is a Greek word that means "studying the mysteries" of our faith.)
5. At the end of the initiation journey, the person began a responsible Christian life.

Living a "Christian life" means living the way Jesus did. By looking at and listening to Jesus in the gospel stories and during the Eucharistic liturgy, we and those we teach can gradually come to know him and his message better. A key aspect of this message is thanksgiving; other aspects include compassion for those who suffer; helping the poor, the sick, and the imprisoned; and sharing with those in need. Jesus challenges us to be light for the world through our words and actions. In this program, you will guide children in this process, introducing them to a lifelong practice of celebrating the Eucharistic liturgy.

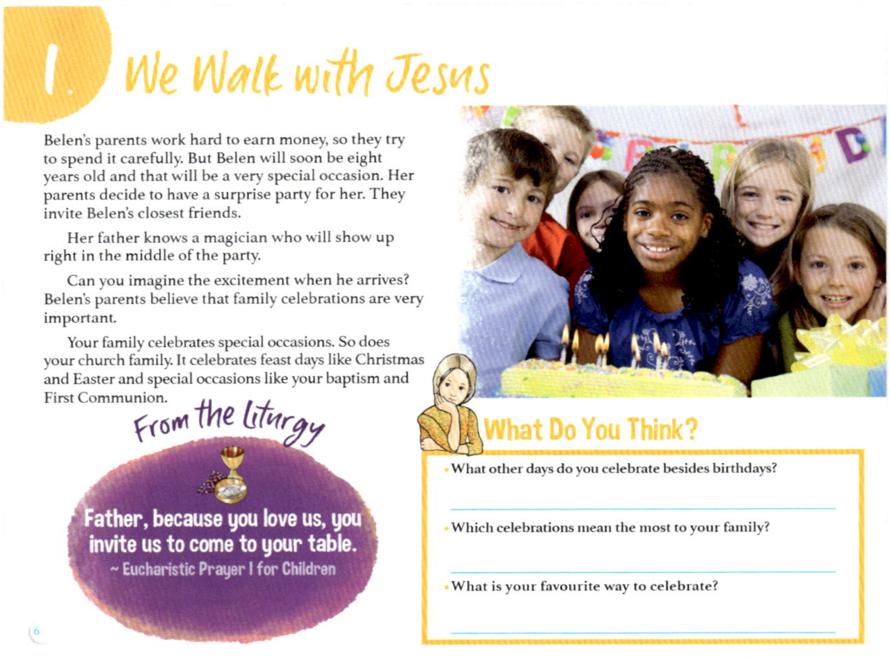

1. We Walk with Jesus

Belen's parents work hard to earn money, so they try to spend it carefully. But Belen will soon be eight years old and that will be a very special occasion. Her parents decide to have a surprise party for her. They invite Belen's closest friends.

Her father knows a magician who will show up right in the middle of the party.

Can you imagine the excitement when he arrives? Belen's parents believe that family celebrations are very important.

Your family celebrates special occasions. So does your church family. It celebrates feast days like Christmas and Easter and special occasions like your baptism and First Communion.

From the Liturgy

Father, because you love us, you invite us to come to your table.
~ Eucharistic Prayer I for Children

What Do You Think?

- What other days do you celebrate besides birthdays?
- Which celebrations mean the most to your family?
- What is your favourite way to celebrate?

6

THEME: *We Walk with Jesus*

FOCUS: **Jesus issues a very special invitation.**

GOAL **To assure the children that God invites them to prepare for First Communion**

- Invite the children to focus on page 6, "We Walk with Jesus." Read the first paragraph. Point out that Belen's parents have to be careful with their money, but they believe that family celebrations are worth the extra expense. Ask the children to describe how Belen looks in the picture. If you have time, invite them to talk about their own recent birthdays. How did they celebrate? Did they remember to thank their parents?
- Read the rest of the text and share the "What Do You Think?" questions. You may need to offer suggestions about occasions the children celebrate with their family: for example, the first day of school, Thanksgiving, Christmas, Easter, birthdays, anniversaries, and graduations.
- Read aloud the "From the Liturgy" words. Ask what "table" is referred to here. If they don't know, explain that the table at church is called the altar. They will receive communion from this special table.

A Day to Remember

After Jesus died on the cross, Peter, Andrew, and all the followers of Jesus gathered together. They were very sad. Jesus was their best friend. He taught them about God's Law of Love and showed them how to live it.

Suddenly, some women ran into the room. Early that morning, before sunrise, they had gone to the tomb where Jesus was buried. Now they had some incredible news.

The tomb was empty! Then the words of Jesus came back to them: "On the third day, I will rise again." They were so happy! Jesus had risen, just as he had said.

Imagine yourself in the place of Peter. He was sad when Jesus died on the cross, but now was filled with joy. Can you remember a time when you were so happy you could hardly speak? It must have been like that for Peter and the others.

THEME: *A Day to Remember*

FOCUS: **The resurrection of Jesus is the greatest celebration of all!**

GOAL **To help the children understand the key events in the life of Jesus (which the Church celebrates, just as families celebrate special events)**

- Ask one of the children to read the first paragraph. Look at the first illustration together. How do the followers look? Have the children ever been through a loss, such as moving to a new city or town, the death of a pet, or the death of a grandparent? How did they feel?
- Ask a second child to read the next paragraph. Then focus on the second illustration. How did the women change the mood? What kind of news did they bring?
- Read the third paragraph in a dramatic way. All of a sudden, the followers remember the promise Jesus made. Ask the children to repeat that promise. Have them look at the third illustration. Invite them to describe it, then together proclaim these words: "He is risen. Alleluia! Alleluia!" Explain that *Alleluia* is a Church word for "Hurray!"
- Now invite the children to close their eyes as you read the last paragraph. Read it meditatively so they can prayerfully think about a time they experienced great happiness. When they open their eyes, invite them to share some of their happy experiences.

A Meal to Remember

A new life began for the friends of Jesus. Jesus had died on the cross, but God raised him to new life. His friends often talked together about all that Jesus had done and said. They remembered his last meal with them, and his beautiful words came back to them.

Imagine yourself at the table with Jesus and his friends. Put yourself in the picture below.

What would you have said to Jesus about his incredible words? What do you think he meant?

THEME: *A Meal to Remember*

FOCUS: **The followers remembered their special meal with Jesus.**

GOAL **To offer the children the concept that we celebrate the Lord's Supper "in memory" of Jesus**

- Read the first paragraph. Ask the children if they remember something that someone special said to them. What helps them remember it? Who said those special words? What was the occasion? Explain that Jesus' followers remembered the words and deeds of Jesus and often talked about them when they got together. They especially remembered the last meal they shared with him. The Church calls this meal the Last Supper.
- Invite the children to discuss the illustration and the words above it. What is Jesus saying? Ask one of the children to read his words.
- Now read the second paragraph. Invite the children to draw themselves into the illustration and then to write out the words they would say to Jesus. Encourage them to put their thoughts in the form of a prayer.

At the end of the meal, Jesus said: "Do this in memory of me." From then on, when his followers shared the bread and wine, they remembered Jesus, and he was there with them.

Just as Jesus asked, his followers soon began to gather every Sunday, the day of the resurrection, in memory of him. For them, every Sunday was like celebrating Easter all over again.

At first his followers met in homes around a dinner table. But soon there were too many of them. They had to move to larger spaces. As the number of followers grew, they built churches where they could share their faith and love in memory of Jesus.

9

The Church Teaches...

Jesus is really and truly present in Communion. He gives us his body and blood.
– adapted for children from Catechism of the Catholic Church (CCC) #1375

- Read the first paragraph, then ask the children if they understand the word "memory." Share how memory can refer to "remembering" or "memorizing" something, but it can also refer to something precious we keep in our hearts. Share this example: Emma went to visit her sick grandmother, whom she loved very much. Her grandmother said to her, "Emma, I love you, and I want you to have the locket I was given when I was a young girl." Soon after that day, her grandmother died, but whenever Emma took out the locket, her memory of her grandmother was very strong. She could feel her grandmother's love.
- Explain to the children that this is how the followers remembered Jesus. Whenever they broke the bread and drank the wine, they could feel the presence of Jesus and they remembered his words: "This is my body; this is my blood. Do this in memory of me."
- Ask a child to read paragraph two. Ask why Sunday was so special for Jesus' followers (*because Jesus rose from the dead on a Sunday*). Turn back to the illustration of the risen Jesus on page 7. Explain that we celebrate the resurrection of Jesus at Easter, but every Sunday is like a little Easter for the Church. Every Sunday, we remember the Last Supper and the resurrection.

A Prayer for You

Dear Jesus, here I am preparing children
to learn about the Eucharist.
It is a mystery to me how you are present
in the sharing of your body and blood,
but I believe you are there,
and I want those I teach to believe it, too.
Open my mind and heart to you.
that I will remember your words and deeds,
and guide me as I try to share them.
Amen.

- Explain that there were no Christian churches in Jesus' time. Where do the children think his followers gathered? Encourage them to discuss this question. Then read the third paragraph and invite the children to look at the church. Does it look like their parish church? How is it different?

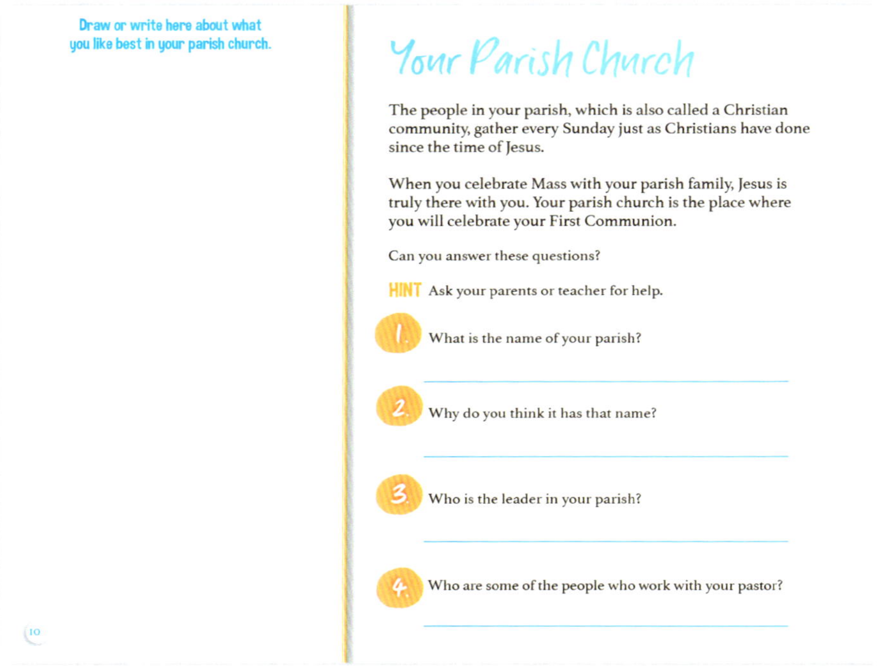

Draw or write here about what you like best in your parish church.

10

Your Parish Church

The people in your parish, which is also called a Christian community, gather every Sunday just as Christians have done since the time of Jesus.

When you celebrate Mass with your parish family, Jesus is truly there with you. Your parish church is the place where you will celebrate your First Communion.

Can you answer these questions?

HINT Ask your parents or teacher for help.

1. What is the name of your parish?
2. Why do you think it has that name?
3. Who is the leader in your parish?
4. Who are some of the people who work with your pastor?

THEME: *Your Parish Church*

FOCUS: **Memory is a powerful gift that takes us into mysteries too deep to explain.**

GOAL **To help the children focus on the parish church as the place to remember Jesus**

- Read the first paragraph on page 10. Be sure the children understand that going to Mass and gathering as Christians are not new. We who believe in Jesus gather to remember him just as his early followers did. We gather in our parish church.
- Help the children fill in the answers to the questions about their parish. (If there are children who do not go to a particular church, have them write in the answers for your parish.) Then point out the shape of the church. Invite them to draw something about their parish church that they really love. For example: the people who gather; the candles, cross, statues, altar, windows, high ceiling, etc. (Children who do not go to a particular church can draw something they would like to see in a church.)

1. What Have You Learned?

See how well you have listened and learned. Use these words to answer the questions below:

Communion, memory, Sunday, Mass, Jesus, Easter

1. ______________ is the greatest Christian feast day.
2. It is the day God raised ______________ to new life.
3. During his last meal, Jesus said: "Do this in ______________ of me."
4. After the Resurrection, the friends of Jesus began to meet on ______________.
5. At ______________, the members of your parish family share the Bread of Life.
6. When you celebrate your First ______________, you will also share the Bread of Life.

From the Bible

Jesus taught his followers God's Law of Love. Here is how the Bible describes it: "You shall love the Lord your God with all your heart, and with all your soul, and with all your might."
~ Deuteronomy 6:5

At the Last Supper, Jesus taught his followers this new law of love: "Love one another as I have loved you."
~ adapted from John 15:12

Let us Pray

Invite your family to say this prayer before meals with you:

Lord Jesus, bless this meal
that we are about to share,
and please bless all the people in our world
who are hungry this day. Amen.

11

THEME: What Have You Learned?

FOCUS: We walk with Jesus.

GOAL To help the children review and discuss what they have learned so far

- Review the words the children will use to answer the six questions. Say each word and have the children repeat after you. Then invite them to find the correct word for each sentence. When all have completed the task, go over each sentence and have the children repeat it after you.
- Focus on the "From the Bible" words. First look at those from the Old Testament, then look at the gospel words. Explain that Jesus asks us to remember him, but also to remember the teachings of the Bible and of the Church. Have the children take turns reading these words aloud several times.
- If possible, have a copy of the "Let us Pray" words and prayer for each child to take home to use for a meal prayer. Pray it together in class beginning with the Sign of the Cross. Have the children close their eyes and fold their hands as they repeat the words after you.

A Prayer for You

All you holy angels and saints of God
and Mary, my mother,
I ask you to pray for the children in my class.
Ask God to give them faith,
to open their minds to the new things
they are learning,
and to teach them how to pray.
These children are so simple and beautiful,
so trusting that I will lead them
on the right path.
Watch over me and guide me as I teach them.
May I lead them to the heart of Jesus.
Amen.

2. We Learn About the Mass

When you go to Mass, also called the celebration of the Lord's Supper, or the celebration of the Eucharist, you look, you listen, you sing, and you make gestures. You watch what the priest does as he leads the people in prayer. But it is *all of us together* who celebrate the Eucharist. The two main parts of the Mass are the **Liturgy of the Word** and the **Liturgy of the Eucharist**.

This book is called the Lectionary.

The Parts of the Mass

The Gathering

- The people arrive, greet one another, and gather in response to God's call
- The priest enters with servers and other ministers and everyone sings
- The priest greets all of us gathered to share the Lord's Supper
- We then pray for forgiveness and we praise God

The Liturgy of the Word

- We listen to the Word of God
- The priest speaks to us to help us better understand the Word of God
- We profess our faith
- We pray for the whole world

The Liturgy of the Eucharist

- We give thanks to God
- We remember the words of Jesus
- We share the Bread of Life and the Cup of his Blood

The Farewell

- The priest blesses us and asks us to love and serve one another
- The priest and others leave in procession and everyone sings

THEME: We learn about the Mass

FOCUS: **The Eucharistic liturgy is meant to enliven our faith and deepen our love.**

GOAL **To introduce the children to the rites and rituals of the Mass**

- Some of the "church" terms here will be difficult for the children, so don't worry if they don't fully understand. Words like *Mass*, the *Lord's Supper*, *Liturgy*, and *Eucharist* will be repeated often in this book. For now, be sure the children grasp the concept of gathering as believers in Jesus.
- Focus on the chart on the right and emphasize the four major points. At every Mass, we 1) gather together, 2) hear God's Word, 3) remember Jesus and share the Lord's Supper, and 4) say goodbye and take God's Law of Love with us into our lives.
- Review the points under these four headings and invite the children to comment or ask questions. Do they remember doing any of these actions at Mass? Make note of which actions they don't remember at all. (Note: *This chart is intended for you and for parents, as an overview of what topics will be covered with the children during the program.*)
- Invite the children to take turns role-playing the first point, under "The Gathering." Then have volunteers line up to role-play the second point: the entry procession (two servers, a reader, and the priest). Have them process to an "altar." The "priest" bows before the altar, the servers stand on either side, and the reader takes a seat (until it's time to read).

  If you have time, have the children process out ("The Farewell"). The "priest" blesses the people and everyone sings as the procession exits.

  For both processions, have the children sing "This Little Light of Mine" or another simple hymn that they know.

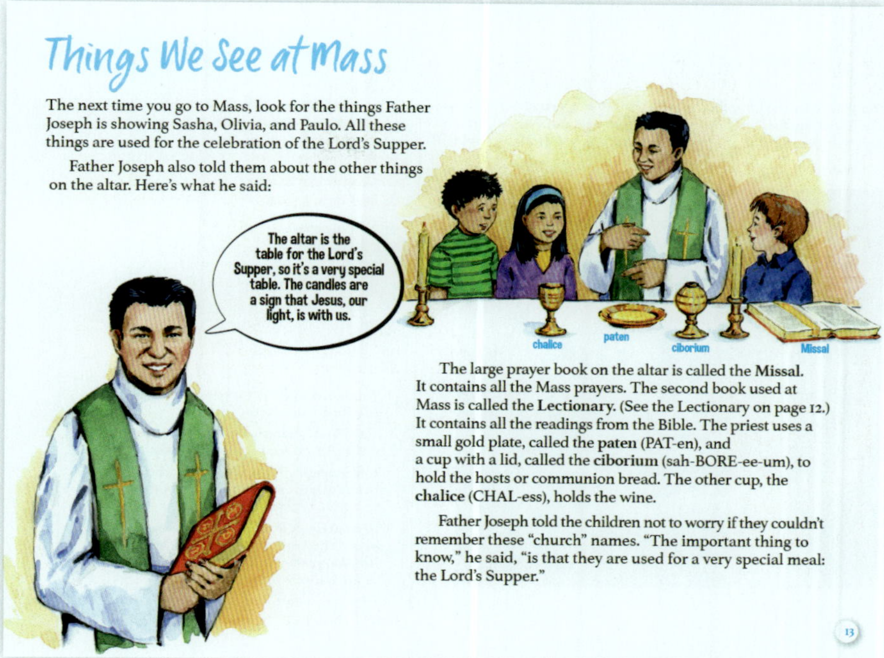

Things We See at Mass

The next time you go to Mass, look for the things Father Joseph is showing Sasha, Olivia, and Paulo. All these things are used for the celebration of the Lord's Supper.

Father Joseph also told them about the other things on the altar. Here's what he said:

The altar is the table for the Lord's Supper, so it's a very special table. The candles are a sign that Jesus, our light, is with us.

chalice

paten

ciborium

Missal

The large prayer book on the altar is called the **Missal.** It contains all the Mass prayers. The second book used at Mass is called the **Lectionary.** (See the Lectionary on page 12.) It contains all the readings from the Bible. The priest uses a small gold plate, called the **paten** (PAT-en), and a cup with a lid, called the **ciborium** (sah-BORE-ee-um), to hold the hosts or communion bread. The other cup, the **chalice** (CHAL-ess), holds the wine.

Father Joseph told the children not to worry if they couldn't remember these "church" names. "The important thing to know," he said, "is that they are used for a very special meal: the Lord's Supper."

13

THEME: Things We See at Mass

FOCUS: **The priest uses many objects (books and vessels) during the Eucharistic liturgy.**

GOAL **To introduce the children to some of the many objects used for the Lord's Supper and increase their interest in them**

- Focus on the illustration at the top right of page 13. What items do the children see? Do they remember seeing these at Mass? Read the first paragraph. Before proceeding, say the words that appear in bold print and have the children repeat them after you. (They do not have to memorize these.) Now read the final paragraph. As it indicates, the children are simply being introduced to some of the things they will see at Mass. Allow them to ask questions or make comments about any of these words/objects.
- Invite one of the children to read what Father Joseph says about the altar and the candles.

Notes for Catechists

Involve the Children

Here's how Psalm 47 says we should pray:

"Clap your hands, all you peoples;
shout to God with loud songs of joy."

Psalm 66 says something similar:

"Make a joyful noise to God, all the earth!"

Class activities and prayers should be an experience of spontaneous joy. Encourage the children to participate with their voices, their bodies, and all their might. Repetition is great for children at this age, and role-playing allows them to give expression to what they are learning. The more involved they are, the better!

We Share Greetings

When you enter the church, the priest or other greeters say hello to you to make you feel welcome. People greet one another as they gather. You should also greet those around you before Mass begins.

At the beginning of Mass, the priest greets everyone from the altar, saying:
The grace of our Lord Jesus Christ,
and the love of God,
and the communion of the
Holy Spirit be with you all.

Everyone answers:
And with your spirit.

Did You Know?

- You are invited to say the Mass prayers in a loud, clear voice.
- The Mass has been the special prayer of Christians for two thousand years.
- It is a custom in the Church for the priest to wear special garments called vestments at Mass.
- Several times during Mass the priest says, "The Lord be with you." What do you answer? (Check your answer at the bottom of the page.)

ANSWER: And with your spirit.

14

THEME: *We Share Greetings*

FOCUS: **Before we begin the official prayer of the Church, we greet one another with love.**

GOAL **To introduce the children to the gathering rite at Sunday Mass**

- Draw attention to the illustration at the bottom left of page 14. Ask the children to interpret what they see. Does anyone greet them when they arrive for Mass? Who is it? What does the person say?
- Read the first paragraph. Ask the children if they say hello to people when they arrive in the church. Why or why not? Explain that the priest always greets the people at the beginning of Mass with these special words: "The grace of our Lord Jesus Christ, and the love of God, and the communion of the Holy Spirit be with you all." Everyone answers, "And with your spirit." Invite the children to take turns being the priest and proclaiming this greeting. All give the response. When all have had a turn, say it once more yourself and invite the children to respond loudly and clearly.
- Go over the "Did You Know?" statements. Be sure the children understand by having them repeat the statements after you. Then ask a few questions:
  - — How should you respond to the prayers at Mass?
  - — For whom is the Mass a special prayer?
  - — Who are Christians?
  - — What special garments does the priest wear?
  - — When the priest says, "The Lord be with you," how do you answer?

Notes for Catechists

Show a Little Life!

Don't be afraid to be a "fool for Christ" when you teach. Be dramatic, exaggerate your facial expressions, speak in a loud, clear voice, and use bodily gestures. You want your message to reach eyes and ears, but also hearts! Encourage the children to role-play dramatically, to say prayer words enthusiastically, and to participate fully.

We Are a Family

When we come to Mass, we join Catholics all over the world in worship. We sing, we make gestures, we stand and kneel. We pray the same prayers in many different languages. We ask God to take care of the poor and the suffering. We all gather in memory of Jesus. How lucky we are to be called to the Lord's Table!

The Church Teaches...

At Mass we share our faith in the real presence of Christ.
~ adapted for children from CCC #1382

Let us Pray

Praise God with shouts of joy, all people!
Sing to the glory of God's name.

~ adapted from Psalm 42:4

15

THEME: *We Are a Family*

FOCUS: **When we gather at Mass, we join Christians all over the world.**

GOAL **To help the children understand that they are part of one great global family**

- Ask the children to describe what they see in the illustration. Do they know any of these people? What do they have in common? (Let them guess.) Now read the first paragraph. Talk about the five things we have in common with Catholics all over the world:
  1. we come to Mass for worship (respect and admiration for God expressed through the rites and prayers of the Mass);
  2. we participate by singing, standing, kneeling;
  3. we pray the same Mass prayers (every country in its own language);
  4. we remember the poor and the suffering;
  5. we gather in memory of Jesus.

  Do the children remember doing some of these things at Mass?
- Focus on "The Church Teaches." This statement offers yet another way to express what we share with believers all over the world at Mass. Proclaim this statement dramatically and have the children repeat it after you.
- Explain to the children that we always pray one of the psalms at Mass. Psalms are sacred hymns that praise God, seek help, express sorrow, and more. They are found in the Bible. King David wrote some (but not all) of them. Ask the children to fold their hands and bow their heads for prayer. Pray the "Let us Pray" words and encourage the children to think about their meaning. Then have them repeat the words after you.

We Ask Forgiveness

Once upon a time, there was a little prince who came from a faraway planet. One day he met a very wise fox in the desert. The fox explained to the little prince that before you meet a friend, you must "dress up your heart."

★ ☆ ★

This is just what you do at Mass before meeting the Lord. You quiet your heart and ask yourself, "Have I dressed up my heart by praying, doing good for others, and giving up my bad habits?"

The priest says: **Brothers and sisters, let us acknowledge our sins, and so prepare ourselves to celebrate the sacred mysteries.**

The people remain silent for a few moments and then praise God for the gift of forgiveness by chanting these words: **Lord, have mercy. Christ, have mercy. Lord, have mercy.**

In Greek, the words are *Kyrie eleison* (keer-ee-AY a-LAY-ee-sahn) and *Christe eleison* (kris-TAY a-LAY-ee-sahn). Sometimes parishes use these words in the chant. When you say them you are speaking a little Greek!

Then the priest says: **May almighty God have mercy on us, forgive us our sins, and bring us to everlasting life.**

We answer: **Amen!**

16

THEME: *We Ask Forgiveness*

FOCUS: **When we go to meet a friend, it is good to "dress up our hearts."**

GOAL **To share with the children how the liturgy celebrates God's forgiveness**

- Read the first paragraph. Ask the children if they have ever heard of a book called *The Little Prince*. (Read this little book beforehand; it's as much for adults as for children. Most libraries have it.) The fox in the story teaches the Little Prince how to form a special friendship. Ask the children if they ever get "dressed up." For what occasions? What might it mean to dress up their heart? *(answers could include: to be excited about meeting a friend; to look forward to it; to treat friends with great respect; to realize that friendship is a gift)*
- Now share the second paragraph. Explain to the children that preparing for their First Communion is one way they are "dressing up their hearts" to meet Jesus in a new way.
- Explain that at Mass, we have time to stop and think about what is in our hearts. We ask God to forgive us if we have done wrong. Most of all, we celebrate God's love and forgiveness. Now read the dialogue between the priest and the people. Ask the children to take turns being the priest.

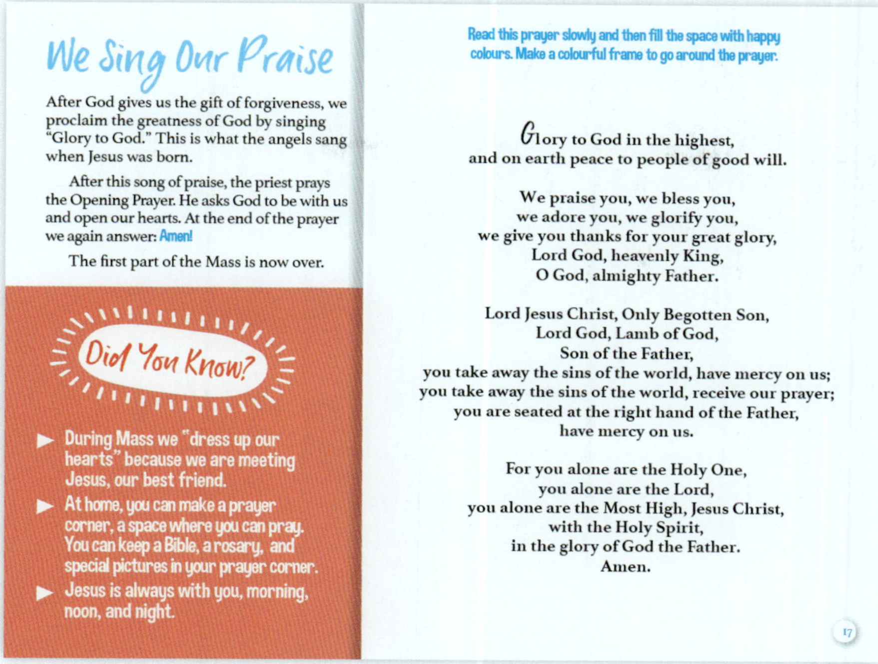

We Sing Our Praise

After God gives us the gift of forgiveness, we proclaim the greatness of God by singing "Glory to God." This is what the angels sang when Jesus was born.

After this song of praise, the priest prays the Opening Prayer. He asks God to be with us and open our hearts. At the end of the prayer we again answer: Amen!

The first part of the Mass is now over.

Did You Know?

- During Mass we "dress up our hearts" because we are meeting Jesus, our best friend.
- At home, you can make a prayer corner, a space where you can pray. You can keep a Bible, a rosary, and special pictures in your prayer corner.
- Jesus is always with you, morning, noon, and night.

Read this prayer slowly and then fill the space with happy colours. Make a colourful frame to go around the prayer.

Glory to God in the highest,
and on earth peace to people of good will.

We praise you, we bless you,
we adore you, we glorify you,
we give you thanks for your great glory,
Lord God, heavenly King,
O God, almighty Father.

Lord Jesus Christ, Only Begotten Son,
Lord God, Lamb of God,
Son of the Father,
you take away the sins of the world, have mercy on us;
you take away the sins of the world, receive our prayer;
you are seated at the right hand of the Father,
have mercy on us.

For you alone are the Holy One,
you alone are the Lord,
you alone are the Most High, Jesus Christ,
with the Holy Spirit,
in the glory of God the Father.
Amen.

17

THEME: We Sing Our Praise

FOCUS: **We share a happy song of praise called the Glory to God (the Gloria).**

GOAL **To explore our song of praise at Mass and to talk more about places where the children can pray**

- Share with the children that once we have asked God's forgiveness and dressed up our hearts, we all share a happy song of praise called the Glory to God. The first part of this song uses the words the angels sang on the night Jesus was born. Have children pray this now, in full voice, line by line after you (as on page 17). Invite them to hold open their hands as they pray.
- After this song of praise, the priest prays a formal prayer called the Opening Prayer. All respond, "Amen." This prayer concludes the first part of the Mass. To illustrate how we use the word "amen" to say, "Yes, I believe it" to something, ask children to loudly pray "Amen" to these statements:

— At Mass we come together to praise and thank God!

— God forgives us when we fail and helps us to do better!

— When we pray, we are talking to God about our lives!

— When we say "Amen" to the prayers at Mass, we are saying, "Yes, I believe it."

- Take time now to review the "Did You Know?" questions. Engage the children in conversation. Do they understand what it means to "dress up their hearts"? Have them share times when they have done this. Do any of them have prayer corners at home, or a space where they go to pray? Would they like such a space? Why or why not? What would they keep there? What helps them to pray? Do they believe that Jesus is always with them? (Be sure they understand that Jesus is present in spirit and not as a physical person or presence.)

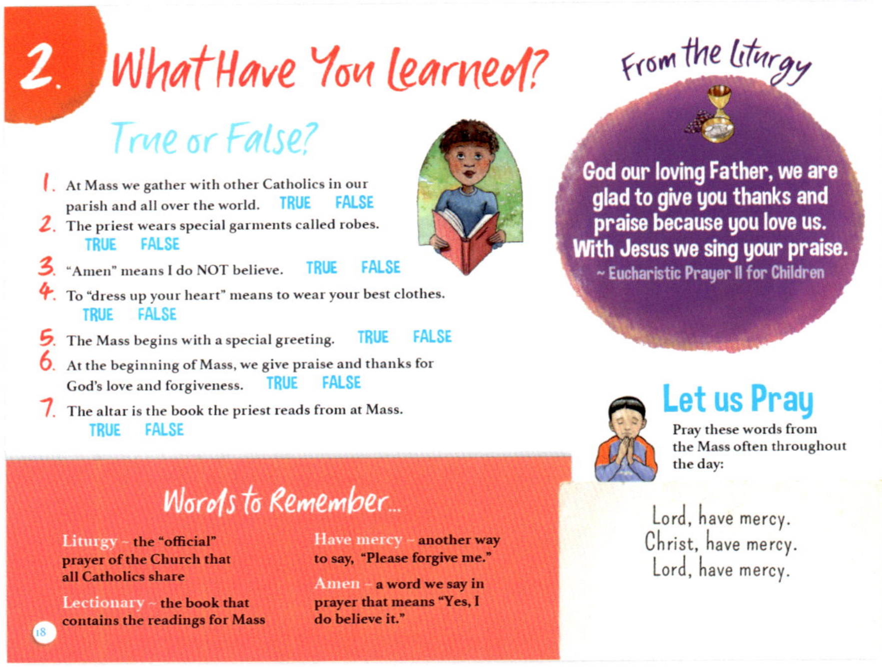

2. What Have You Learned?

True or False?

1. At Mass we gather with other Catholics in our parish and all over the world. TRUE FALSE
2. The priest wears special garments called robes. TRUE FALSE
3. "Amen" means I do NOT believe. TRUE FALSE
4. To "dress up your heart" means to wear your best clothes. TRUE FALSE
5. The Mass begins with a special greeting. TRUE FALSE
6. At the beginning of Mass, we give praise and thanks for God's love and forgiveness. TRUE FALSE
7. The altar is the book the priest reads from at Mass. TRUE FALSE

Words to Remember...

Liturgy – the "official" prayer of the Church that all Catholics share

Lectionary – the book that contains the readings for Mass

Have mercy – another way to say, "Please forgive me."

Amen – a word we say in prayer that means "Yes, I do believe it."

18

From the Liturgy

God our loving Father, we are glad to give you thanks and praise because you love us. With Jesus we sing your praise.
~ Eucharistic Prayer II for Children

Let us Pray

Pray these words from the Mass often throughout the day:

Lord, have mercy.
Christ, have mercy.
Lord, have mercy.

THEME: What Have You Learned?

FOCUS: We learn about the Mass.

GOAL To help the children review and discuss what they have learned in Theme 2

- Read the "True or False?" statements aloud. Invite the children to call out the answers. Go over any statements they seem uncertain about.
- Now look at the "Words to Remember." The first three are difficult concepts, so have the children guess what the words mean and describe them in their own words. Read the definitions and give examples.

— An example of a liturgy is the Mass.

— The lectionary is the big book the reader carries in the procession at the start of Mass.

— We say "Have mercy" at the beginning of Mass

Point out the "Let us Pray" words. Have the children fold their hands and repeat each line after you. Show them how the phrase "Have mercy" (from "Words to Remember") connects with this prayer. Finally, remind them that "Amen" means "Yes!"

- Explain to the children that the words "From the Liturgy" are prayed during Mass. Ask:

— What does this prayer call God?

— What are we "glad" to give God?

— Who helps us to sing God's praises?

Now invite the children to share ways they might sing God's praises at home and at school.

3. We Share God's Word

At Mass, a person called a **lector** or **reader** proclaims words from the Bible. The Bible is a very special book that tells about God's great love for us. It also tells about people who lived long ago and who had great faith in God. When we read or hear stories from the Bible, we are learning the history of Jesus. This history also becomes our story because we are the followers of Jesus.

19

THEME: *We Share God's Word*

FOCUS: **God's Word calls us to wisdom and understanding, peace, joy, and love.**

GOAL **To introduce the children to some of the great people in the Bible**

- Ask the children to comment on the illustration. What do they see? Why do they think this is called the "People of Faith Gallery"? Have any of them ever been to an art museum or gallery? What did they see? What do they remember most?
- Read the paragraph at the top of the page. Do the children remember seeing and hearing the readers in their own parish? Remind them that the reader walks in with the priest, holding high the lectionary, the big book that contains the readings. The reader goes to the ambo to "proclaim" the Scripture reading.
- Show the children a Bible. Let them see how large it is. Explain that the stories about the people in the "People of Faith Gallery" are found in the Bible. Sometimes at Mass we listen to parts of their stories. All the readings at Mass come from the Bible.

We Learn About the Bible

Some of the people you saw in the People of Faith Gallery were leaders of the Jewish people. They were ancestors of Jesus, and he learned about them when he was a child. When you read the Bible, you can learn about them, too. Here is part of the story.

At the time of Abraham, people believed in many different gods and worshipped them all. But God asked Abraham to be the father of a new people who would worship the one true God. Abraham moved to a new land as God asked. There he and his wife, Sarah, had a son named Isaac. Abraham followed the paths of God. He spoke to God as a friend.
He taught Isaac to do the same.

THEME: *We learn about the Bible*

FOCUS: **Jesus studied the Bible as a child and learned about his ancestors there.**

GOAL **To help children see the Bible as a way to learn about its major religious figures**

- Read the first paragraph. Emphasize that Jesus learned about these Bible people when he was a child. He probably knew the story of Abraham by heart.
- Share the story of Abraham by "proclaiming" paragraph two. Explain to the children that you are not just reading, you are saying these words in a special way. Ask: What do you think of Abraham? What does it mean to follow the paths of God? How did Abraham speak to God?
- Focus on the illustrations. Ask the children to explain what they see. Why did God want Abraham to move? Was it easy or difficult for people to move to a new land in those days?

A Prayer for You

Lord Jesus, you are challenging me
to unlock the truth of your Word
for and with those I teach.
But first I need to unlock it within myself,
to open the eyes of my own heart,
that I might truly and deeply know you.
Please turn the rusty key of my faith
and understanding,
that I might recognize you once again
as if for the first time.
I do long to know you better.
I do want to share your presence
with those I teach.
May I proclaim your Word so fully,
and be so strong in my convictions,
that their hearts, too, will open,
and together we can pray...
"You are the Christ, the Son of the Living God,
both now and forever.
Amen."

Later, some of Isaac's children and grandchildren moved to the land of Egypt where they could get food. But after many years, the leader there decided to make them slaves. Their lives were very hard. Then God called Moses to lead the people out of Egypt back to their own land. Moses did as God asked, but it took 40 years for the people to return home. During that time, God gave Moses this Law of Love:

"You shall love the Lord your God with all your heart, and with all your soul, and with all your might."

~Deuteronomy 6:5

21

- Read the first paragraph loudly and clearly. Have the children ever heard of Moses? What do they remember? How do they think Moses felt to be given such a difficult task? Explain that the people were in the desert for 40 years before they found a new land. During that time, they became restless and impatient. They decided to turn away from God. They made a golden calf and said, "Let this be our god!" Moses became very angry with them, because he always kept God's Law of Love in his heart.
- Now read the passage from Deuteronomy and have the children repeat it after you. Then invite each child to take turns proclaiming it. Explain that Jesus learned this Law of Love when he was a child and would have recited it every day.
- Have the children study the illustration and comment on it. What do they see? Who do they see?
- Send a note home encouraging parents and child to watch the movie *The Prince of Egypt*, an animated story about Moses and his mission.

Notes for Catechists

The Ten Commandments

You might want to share with the children that when Moses and the people were in the desert, God gave him the Ten Commandments. Here is a version for children.

1. Love God with all your heart.
2. Do not curse or swear.
3. Remember that Sunday is a holy day.
4. Love and respect your parents.
5. Respect all life.
6. Be a good and faithful husband or wife.
7. Do not steal from others.
8. Do not tell lies.
9. Do not be jealous of what others have.
10. Respect your neighbour and all that is theirs.

—*adapted from Exodus 20:1-21*

When Jesus' ancestors arrived back in their land, they formed a kingdom to keep order. Their leader was King David. Like Abraham and Moses, David taught his people to love and serve one God.

To tell God of his faith and love, David wrote beautiful prayers that we call the **psalms**. We sing one of the psalms every Sunday at Mass.

When the people forgot about God, others, called **prophets**, reminded them to turn back to God. The prophet Isaiah made this important announcement:

Then came John the Baptist, the cousin of Jesus. He prepared the way for Jesus.

- Read the first two paragraphs. Explain that once the people reached the land God had promised them, also known as the Promised Land, they needed a leader. (Moses died just before they arrived.) David, a shepherd boy, became their king. David often praised God by writing songs called psalms. (You might want to read aloud Psalm 23, "The Lord Is My Shepherd.")
- Ask one of the children to look at the illustration on the top right. Who do they think this is? (*David*)What is he doing? (*Perhaps composing or singing one of the psalms.*)
- Ask one of the children to read the third paragraph. Explain that prophets are people who speak in the name of God. Isaiah was a great prophet who told the people to change their ways and to turn their hearts to God and God's Law of Love.
- Ask the children to focus on the illustration of Isaiah on the left. What is he saying? Have each child take a turn being Isaiah and proclaiming his words.
- Ask one of the children to read the last paragraph. Now have the children look at the illustration of John. What do they think he is doing? Who do they think he is talking about?
- Have the children now turn back to page 19. Ask them to make believe that they are in this "People of Faith Gallery" as guides. Choose five children to be guides: each tells the group something about one of the persons pictured. Then give a turn to the next five children, inviting them to add something to what was already said. Continue until each child has been a guide. Sum up by reminding the children that each of these people came before Jesus, and Jesus learned from all of them. Each is a famous person in the Bible who prepared the way for Jesus.

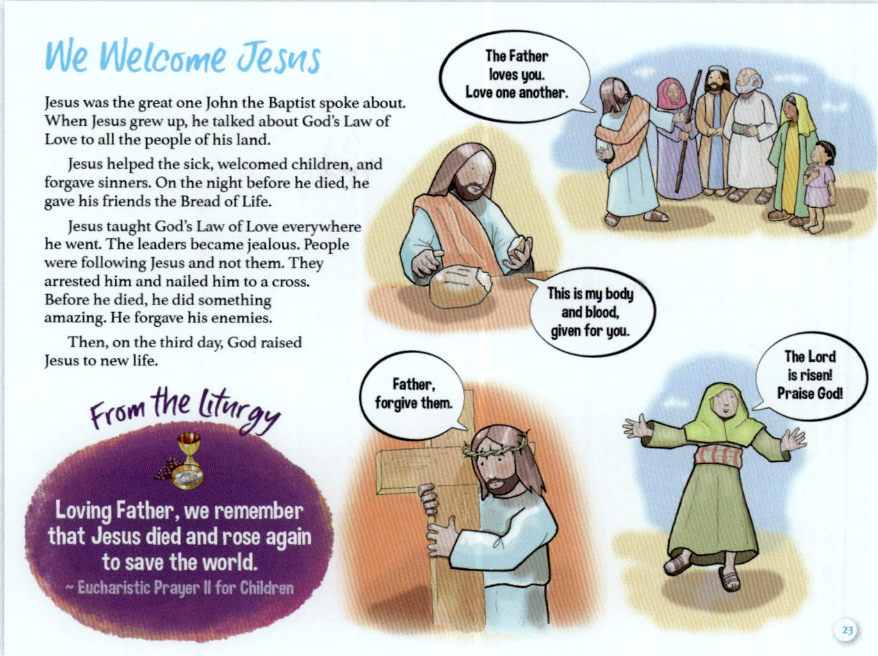

We Welcome Jesus

Jesus was the great one John the Baptist spoke about. When Jesus grew up, he talked about God's Law of Love to all the people of his land.

Jesus helped the sick, welcomed children, and forgave sinners. On the night before he died, he gave his friends the Bread of Life.

Jesus taught God's Law of Love everywhere he went. The leaders became jealous. People were following Jesus and not them. They arrested him and nailed him to a cross. Before he died, he did something amazing. He forgave his enemies.

Then, on the third day, God raised Jesus to new life.

From the Liturgy

Loving Father, we remember that Jesus died and rose again to save the world.
~ Eucharistic Prayer II for Children

23

THEME: *We Welcome Jesus*

FOCUS: **Jesus is the compassionate face of God who extends God's love and healing to all.**

GOAL **To introduce the children to Jesus' story and prominent place in the Bible**

- Read the first paragraph, then have the children focus on the illustration at the top right. Whom do they see? What is Jesus saying? Have each child proclaim the words of Jesus as they think he might have said them: boldly, quietly, calmly, etc.
- Ask one child to read paragraph two. Explain that these are only a few of the things Jesus did: helped the sick, welcomed children, forgave sinners, and gave his friends the Bread of Life (his body and blood) to share in memory of him.
- Ask the children to look at the illustration of Jesus at the Last Supper. What is he doing? What is he saying? Have each child say the words as they think he might have said them. Remind the children that whenever Jesus' followers broke the bread and drank the wine, they could feel the presence of Jesus and they remembered his words: "This is my body; this is my blood given for you. Do this in memory of me." We, too, remember this action at every Mass.
- Now ask a child to read paragraph three, and then the words of Jesus from the cross. Ask the children to bow their heads, close their eyes, and thank Jesus for the gift of forgiveness, in their own words and in silence.
- Ask a child to read paragraph four. Look at the "From the Liturgy" words. Proclaim them and then have the children take turns proclaiming them. Everyone can answer "Alleluia!" after each repetition.

After his resurrection, Jesus appeared several times to his friends. They were amazed and filled with joy. Jesus told them he was returning to his Father. Before he left, he asked them to share God's Law of Love with everyone. Then he promised to send them the Holy Spirit.

As Jesus' followers and his mother waited for the Spirit, they were praying together. Suddenly a great gust of wind filled the house. Flashes of fire touched each one of them but did not burn them.

They were all filled with the Holy Spirit. The Holy Spirit gave them courage. Peter and the others began at once to spread the news about Jesus. They told everyone: "Love one another as Jesus loved you."

A few years later, a man named Saul was on his way to arrest everyone who believed in Jesus. On the road to Damascus, Saul met the risen Christ. From that moment on, Saul became a follower. He changed his name to Paul and became a great missionary, spreading the news about Jesus everywhere he went.

The Church Teaches...

Be merciful and forgiving, as Jesus was, and love others as he has loved us.

– adapted for children from CCC #2842

- Read paragraph one. Ask the children if they know what promise Jesus made. (He told them he would soon send the Holy Spirit.) Direct them now to the illustration of the disciples and Mary. What do they see? Do they think this was a happy time or a scary time? Why?
- Now read paragraphs two and three. Invite the children to do a pantomime of this scene. At first the disciples are quietly praying, and then there is a loud noise and flashes of fire. Encourage the children to express with their bodies and faces how it felt to be there. Then ask: What do you think they told people about Jesus? Proclaim the words "Love one another as Jesus loved you," and have the children repeat them after you. Jesus wanted the disciples to teach God's Law of Love.
- Ask one of the children to read paragraph four. Share with the children Acts 9:1-7, which gives the details about Paul "meeting" the risen Christ. Now focus on the illustration of Paul. Where do they think he was going? What was he going to tell people? Explain that Paul travelled long distances to tell people about Jesus, but he also wrote letters to the people he had visited. Almost every Sunday at Mass, the reader proclaims some of the messages of Paul.
- Ask the children how they can share the story of Jesus with others. What do they think Jesus would want them to do or say? Close by making the Sign of the Cross together, slowly and reverently.

Notes for Catechists

The Way of Jesus

Jesus taught a "way" or path to his followers. His teachings point to an understanding of each person's spiritual life as a journey. He talked about seeking and entering the kingdom or reign of God. These are active words. They involve doing something active: moving from where we are to someplace new.

The Liturgy of the Word

In the first two readings, we listen to the messages of the prophets and apostles. They tell us about God and teach us to follow God's Law of Love. At the end of each reading, the reader says:

The word of the Lord.

All answer:

Thanks be to God.

After the first reading, we sing one of the psalms.

The Lord is compassionate and gracious,
slow to anger, abounding in love.

– adapted from Psalm 103:8

Then we stand to listen to the gospel.
But before it is read, we express our joy by singing, **Alleluia!** which means "Praise the Lord."

The Church Teaches...

The Liturgy of the Word includes the writings of the prophets and the memoirs of the apostles.

– adapted for children from CCC #1349

Did You Know?

- The word Gospel means "good news."
- The Gospels contain the teachings of Jesus.
- There are four Gospels.
- The Gospels are named after their writers: Matthew, Mark, Luke, and John.

25

THEME: *The Liturgy of the Word*

FOCUS: **God speaks to us through the readings and prayers at Mass.**

GOAL **To introduce the children to the Liturgy of the Word and its responses**

- Review with the children that the stories about Abraham, Moses, David, and Isaiah are sometimes read at Mass in the first reading. The letters of Paul are read in the second reading, and the stories and teachings of Jesus are read in the gospel. Then read paragraph one and proclaim the words "The word of the Lord." Have the children respond, "Thanks be to God." Ask if any remember saying this response at Mass. Why do they think we thank God after listening to Scripture?
- Remind the children that King David wrote many of the psalms in the Bible. Every Sunday at Mass, we pray one of the psalms after the first reading. Usually, the psalm is sung.
- Now read the paragraph about the gospel. Do the children remember singing "Alleluia" at Mass? Remind them that the gospel readings are usually about Jesus and his teachings. Go over the "Did You Know?" statements and have the children repeat each one after you. If you have a Bible, show them the section containing the four gospels.
- Ask the children to focus on the illustration. What do they see? How do the children in the picture look? Explain that they, too, should be attentive and participate during the readings and the singing of the responsorial psalm. Now review with them that the first part of the Mass is called the Liturgy of the Word. Then read "The Church Teaches." Remind the children that Isaiah was a prophet. Paul and the four gospel writers wrote the "memoirs of the apostles."

Note: *The Liturgy of the Word is not primarily a "teaching". It is truly God (Jesus) speaking to God's people today (General Instruction of the Roman Missal #55). It is one of the four modes of "real presence" spoken of in the Council and in the GIRM.*

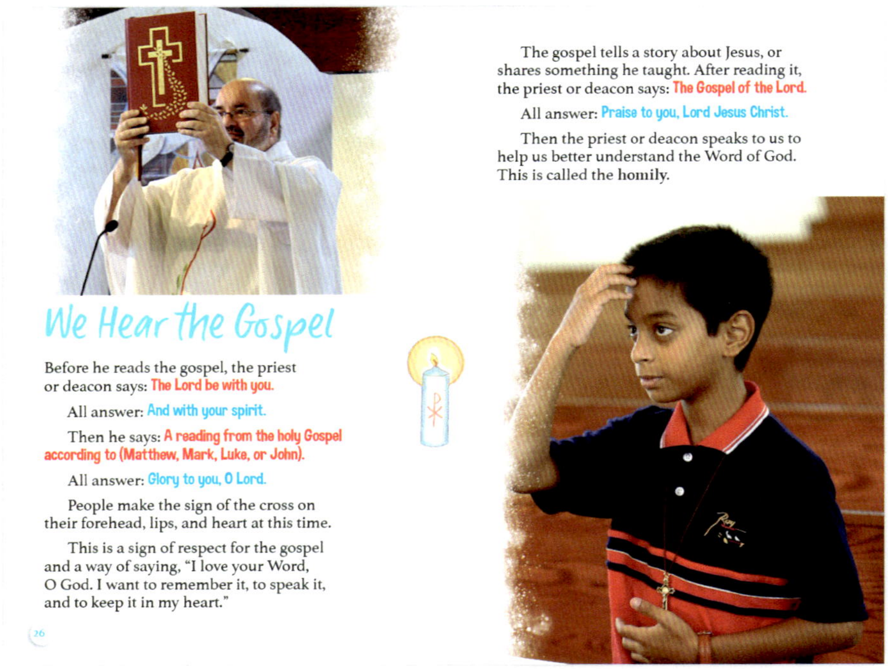

We Hear the Gospel

Before he reads the gospel, the priest or deacon says: **The Lord be with you.**

All answer: **And with your spirit.**

Then he says: **A reading from the holy Gospel according to (Matthew, Mark, Luke, or John).**

All answer: **Glory to you, O Lord.**

People make the sign of the cross on their forehead, lips, and heart at this time.

This is a sign of respect for the gospel and a way of saying, "I love your Word, O God. I want to remember it, to speak it, and to keep it in my heart."

The gospel tells a story about Jesus, or shares something he taught. After reading it, the priest or deacon says: **The Gospel of the Lord.**

All answer: **Praise to you, Lord Jesus Christ.**

Then the priest or deacon speaks to us to help us better understand the Word of God. This is called the **homily**.

THEME: *We Hear the Gospel*

FOCUS: **The Gospel is revered in the liturgy through key words and gestures.**

GOAL **To review with the children how to prepare for the Gospel reading**

- Ask the children to focus on the illustration on the left. What is the priest doing? Do they remember the name of the book the priest is holding? (*the lectionary*)
- Read the first four paragraphs and practise these invitations and responses. Have the children take turns being the priest. When all have had a turn, ask if they have ever noticed people making small crosses on their foreheads, lips, and chest before the gospel is read at Mass. Have them look at the illustration on the right. What is the child doing?
- Now read the next two paragraphs. Show the children how to make the small crosses on their own foreheads, lips, and chests.
- Now read paragraph seven about the gospel. Ask the children if they remember any gospel stories about Jesus (*the good shepherd, blessing the children, healing people, blessing the loaves and fishes, etc.*). Now practise what the priest says to introduce the gospel, and the people's response. Again, allow the children to take turns being the priest. Close by sharing your own favourite story about Jesus.
- Remind the children that after the gospel is read, the priest or deacon speaks to us about the readings to help us understand their meaning for us today. This is called the homily. Invite them to listen carefully to the homily. Even if they don't understand all of it, they are to sit quietly and politely while the priest is speaking.

We Profess Our Faith

Every Sunday after the homily, we name all the things we believe as Christians. The words we use are from the Creed. The word **Creed** means "beliefs." There are two Creeds that can be used during Mass. The longer one is called the **Nicene Creed.** The other is called the **Apostles' Creed.**

The Apostles' Creed

I believe in God, the Father almighty,
Creator of heaven and earth,
and in Jesus Christ, his only Son, our Lord,*
who was conceived by the Holy Spirit,
born of the Virgin Mary,
suffered under Pontius Pilate,
was crucified, died and was buried;
he descended into hell;
on the third day he rose again from the dead;
he ascended into heaven,
and is seated at the right hand of God
the Father almighty;
from there he will come to judge the living and the dead.

I believe in the Holy Spirit,
the holy catholic Church,
the communion of saints,
the forgiveness of sins,
the resurrection of the body,
and life everlasting. Amen.

* We bow at the next two lines.

27

THEME: We Profess Our Faith

FOCUS: When we say we are believers, we must also practise what we believe.

GOAL

To introduce the children to the concept of a creed and praying for others

- Read the paragraph at the top left of the page. At Mass we share the things we believe as Catholics. Proclaim each line of the Creed (at right) and have the children repeat it after you. Explain that some of these words and phrases might be difficult for them to understand because of the grown-up language. That's okay for now, as long as they understand that the Creed is a statement of our beliefs.

A Prayer for You

Jesus, you are the light of the world
from which I draw my light.
Without you, I have no light.
You are the Word of God
from which I draw my teaching.
Without you, I have no words.
You are the way, the truth, and the life
from which I draw my ministry.
Without you, I have nothing to teach.
Share your gifts with me, please,
that I might draw the children I teach
to your light, your Word, your Way.
Amen.

Did You Know?

The word intercession means to pray for another person or situation.

If you could add an intercession at Mass, what would you pray for?

I would pray for

and also for

The Church Teaches...

In the intercessions we pray with the whole Church in heaven and on earth.

- adapted for children from CCC #1354

28

We Pray for Others

People all over the world are God's children. That is why we pray for one another and for the entire human family every week at Mass. These prayers are called **Intercessory Prayers or Prayers of the Faithful.**

During these prayers, we think of what is happening in our world and in our own country. We pray for our Church leaders, for our country's leaders, for the hungry, for the sick, for countries at war, and for all who are suffering in any way. We also pray for those who have died. We ask for the courage to help one another make our world better for all.

The reader prays these prayers and we all answer: Lord, hear our prayer.

This is the end of the Liturgy of the Word.

THEME: We Pray for Others

FOCUS: **The Intercessory Prayers at Mass unite us with people in the church and all over the world.**

GOAL **To help children focus on these prayers and participate in them**

- Read the first and second paragraphs. Do the children remember this part of the Mass? Be sure they understand the concept of the whole Church praying together for people all over the world. Ask: Who are some of our Church leaders? Who are the leaders in our country? Do the children know anyone who is sick? Do they have relatives or neighbours in the military? Do they know anyone who has died?
- Have the children read and filled in the "Did You Know?" section. They can pray for anyone in any of the categories mentioned, or some other intention. Then have each take a turn as the reader and share his or her intercession(s). Use this form: "For my mother, who is looking for a new job"; "For the leader of our country, who must make difficult decisions," etc. All respond, "Lord, hear our prayer."
- Ask the children to focus on the illustration at the bottom. Who is pictured? Why? (Remind the children about the first sentence on this page.) Now read "The Church Teaches." Have the children repeat it after you. Emphasize the words "the whole Church in heaven and on earth."

3. What Have You Learned?

So far, you have learned about the greetings we share at Mass and about the Liturgy of the Word. See if you can finish these sentences:

1. At Mass, we share the W_______ of God.
2. The B_______ tells us the great story of God's love for all people.
3. For Christians, the coming of J_______, his death, and his resurrection are the most important events in this story.
4. With the H_______ S_______ guiding us, we continue to live God's story.

When the priest greets you at Mass saying, "The Lord be with you," what do you answer?

____

____

From the Liturgy

Learn these words by heart and say them often. "Lord, you are holy; you are kind to us and to all. For this we thank you."
~ Eucharistic Prayer III for Children (adapted)

Words to Remember...

Lector ~ person who proclaims words from the Bible at Mass

Psalms ~ prayers from the Bible inspired by King David

Prophets ~ special people who announce God's Law of Love

Alleluia ~ a word that means "praise God"

Homily ~ a talk about God's Word given by the priest or deacon at Mass

Creed ~ beliefs

Intercessory Prayers ~ prayers for all the human family

29

THEME: *What Have You Learned?*
FOCUS: We share God's Word.

GOAL To review what the children have studied in Theme 3

- Go over the four sentences with the children. Do they remember the correct missing words? The answers are: Word, Bible, God, Jesus, Holy Spirit, and "And with your spirit." Read each sentence aloud and have the children repeat it after you. Then have five children read one sentence each.
- Review the "Words to Remember." Be sure the children can define them in their own words. Remind the children that two of the prophets were Isaiah and John the Baptist.
- Focus now on the "From the Liturgy" words. Invite the children to choose one of the three sentences to write out and illustrate. (They can take these pages home for their prayer corner.)
- Divide the class into three groups. Give the first sentence to group 1, the second sentence to group 2, and so on. Invite the children to recite their sentences loudly and clearly. Then switch sentences so that each group ends up reciting all three sentences. Encourage the children to memorize this prayer from the Mass so they can pray it at home with their families.
- The priest, deacon, or bishop may then give a homily: a sermon that draws upon some aspect of the readings or the liturgy of the day. The homily is mandatory on Sundays and Holy Days of Obligation, and is highly encouraged on other days.
- On Sundays and solemnities, all then profess their Christian faith by reciting or singing the Nicene Creed or, especially from Easter to Pentecost, the Apostles' Creed, which is particularly associated with baptism and often used with Masses for children.
- The Liturgy of the Word concludes with the General intercessions or "Prayers of the Faithful." The congregation responds to each intercession with a phrase such as "Lord, hear our prayer."

4. We Give Thanks

Alicia and Kieran's grandmother bakes her own bread. She knows that Alicia and Kieran love to eat it fresh out of the oven.

What a treat! Thanks for baking this for us.

Ooh, strawberry jam, too. Thanks, Grandma. It's delicious!

While they were eating, Grandma told them how bread is made and how much work and time it takes from start to finish. The farmer plants wheat. When it is grown, the farmer collects the grain and takes it to the mill. There it is ground into flour. Grandma uses the flour to make the bread dough.

30

THEME: We Give Thanks

FOCUS: Wheat and grapes combine to create a royal feast: the Lord's Supper.

GOAL To introduce the children to the Offertory rites

- Focus first on the illustration. Have the children describe it in their own words. What do they think is happening? Now read the story. Have the children ever had fresh-baked bread? Have they ever seen wheat growing (in person, or in a picture)? How does wheat become flour?

  Look together at the photograph of the wheat. Point out that the grain is at the top of the plant. This is the part that is ground into flour.

Did You Know?

The Liturgy of the Word

On Sundays and solemnities, there are three Scripture readings. (On other days there are only two.)

- On Sundays, the first reading is from the Old Testament, or the Acts of the Apostles during the Easter season.
- The first reading is followed by a responsorial Psalm. (It is called "responsorial" because the theme is a response to the first reading.)
- The second reading is from the New Testament, typically from one of the letters Paul wrote to the early Christian communities.
- The final reading and high point of the Liturgy of the Word is the proclamation of the Gospel. We sing the Gospel Acclamation first. Everyone stands while the deacon or priest reads the gospel.

Jesus chose bread and wine to give himself to us at Communion because bread and wine are sources of life and joy. Bread satisfies our hunger. Wine is part of our celebrations.

Before the bread and wine are carried to the altar, there is an offertory collection.

People put money in the baskets to help support the work and needs of the parish.

From the beginning, the Church has used some of this money to help people in need.

31

- Ask the children if they know where wine comes from. (*Hint: The same ingredient is used in grape juice.*) Explain that in many cultures, people drink wine (sometimes mixed with water) with meals. When Jesus was a child, wine was used for special occasions and ceremonies, so it was an important part of a meal, at least on those occasions. (See more below.)
- Now read paragraph one. Have the children noticed the wine cruet and the bread at Mass? (Sometimes these are set out at the back or centre aisle of the church before Mass.) Explain that Jesus chose bread and wine because these were used to celebrate the Jewish feast of Passover. (The Last Supper was celebrated on the evening of Passover.)
- Ask one child to read paragraphs two and three. Most children will remember this moment and are eager to put money in the basket. Ask: Why do you think we place money in the collection basket? What is the money used for? Have the children focus on the top right illustration. Explain that when we give money at church, we are helping to pay for things such as light, heat, flowers, air conditioning, cleaning, etc. Encourage the children to save a bit of their own money to put in the offertory basket so it is really a gift from them.
- Ask a child to read paragraph four. Tell the children that many parishes today give part of the offertory money to the needy. This money helps to feed the hungry, for example. Focus on the bottom right illustration. What are these children doing? Who are they helping? Tell the children that when they place their own money in the basket at church, they are helping the poor as well as the parish.

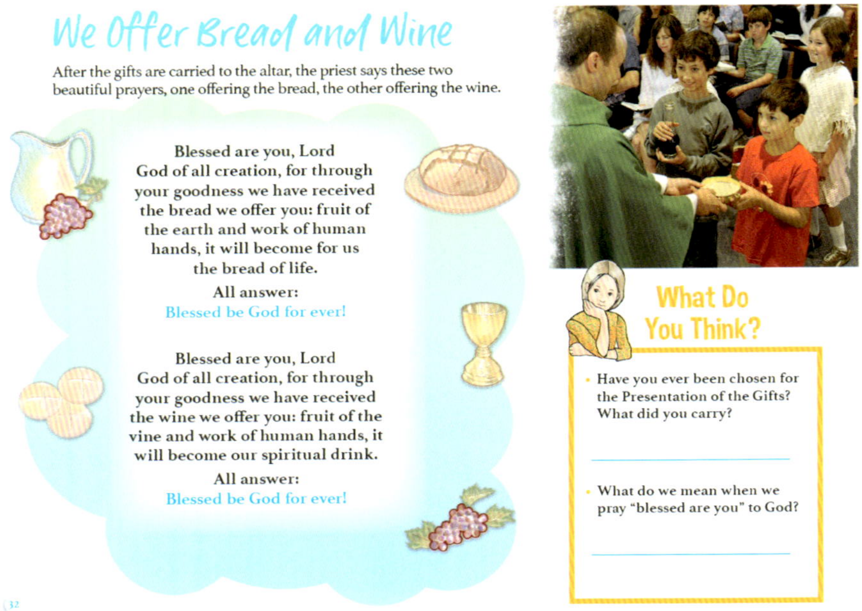
We Offer Bread and Wine

After the gifts are carried to the altar, the priest says these two beautiful prayers, one offering the bread, the other offering the wine.

Blessed are you, Lord God of all creation, for through your goodness we have received the bread we offer you: fruit of the earth and work of human hands, it will become for us the bread of life.

All answer:
Blessed be God for ever!

Blessed are you, Lord God of all creation, for through your goodness we have received the wine we offer you: fruit of the vine and work of human hands, it will become our spiritual drink.

All answer:
Blessed be God for ever!

What Do You Think?

- Have you ever been chosen for the Presentation of the Gifts? What did you carry?
- What do we mean when we pray "blessed are you" to God?

32

THEME: *We Offer Bread and Wine*

FOCUS: The beautiful Offertory prayers remind us that we, too, are being offered to God.

GOAL **To familiarize children with these prayers and to practise responding to them**

- The children will probably recognize the Presentation of the Gifts because it involves action and people from the congregation or assembly. Have them focus on the illustration and invite them to complete the picture.
- Go over the "What Do You Think?" questions. If none of the children have been in the procession before, ask: What would you like to carry? Emphasize that being in the procession is a privilege, because those who carry the gifts are doing so for the whole community. For the second question, tell the children that when we pray "Blessed are you," we are praising God. Ask the children what other words they could use to praise God: for example, great, wonderful, holy, loving, powerful. Or they could say "Alleluia," which means "praise God."
- Explain that the priest says the two prayers during the Presentation of the Gifts. First he offers the bread. "Proclaim" that prayer first, line by line, and have the children repeat it after you. Invite them to speak loudly and clearly and to open their palms and lift their arms. Remind them that this is a prayer. Have them practise the words "Blessed be God for ever!" until they have memorized them. Then give them each a small index card. Have them write these words from memory (with your help, if necessary) and decorate them for their prayer corner at home.

We Lift Our Hearts

After the prayers offering the bread and wine, the priest asks us to pray with him.

The Lord be with you.
All answer:
And with your spirit.

Lift up your hearts.
All answer:
We lift them up to the Lord.

Let us give thanks to the Lord our God.
All answer:
It is right and just.

Do you know what it means to "give thanks" at Mass? It means praising God with love and gratitude. The word Eucharist means "thanksgiving." Mass is a great thanksgiving celebration!

The Thank-you Game

Do you always remember to say thank you?

To help you remember, try playing a Thank-you game with your family or friends.

For three days, all players try to notice and count the number of times in a day that they say "thank you" in a kind way.

At the end of day 3, talk about your thank yous and decide who won.

33

THEME: We Lift Our Hearts

FOCUS: **May we always lift our hearts in glad thanksgiving for all the gifts we receive!**

GOAL **To introduce the children to the importance of prayer and thanksgiving**

- Ask the children if they remember the words of the fox (from *The Little Prince*): before we meet a friend we must "dress up our hearts." Now they have an opportunity in the Mass to "lift up their hearts." Have the children look at the illustration and imitate the gesture of lifting their arms. Explain that this is one way to show that we are lifting our hearts to God.
- Practise the prayers, inviting one child to be the priest. The priest's words are in red type and the responses are in blue. Encourage the children to respond enthusiastically, just as they should do at Mass. Then let them take turns being the priest until all are comfortable with the responses.
- Read the last paragraph on the left. Emphasize the "thanksgiving celebration." Invite the children to say what this means to them. How do they celebrate the holiday of Thanksgiving? *(by gathering with others and sharing a special meal)* This is how Sunday Eucharist (the Mass) is meant to be!
- Go over "The Thank-you Game" information. Encourage the children to do this at home and try to say "thank you" to others often. Also suggest that they say thank you to God often during the day, by visiting their prayer corner or simply by thanking God wherever they happen to be.

The "Great Prayer"

You have already learned that the word **Eucharist** means "thanksgiving." The most important part of the Liturgy of the Eucharist is the great prayer of thanksgiving, which is called the **Eucharistic Prayer**.

The priest leads up to the Eucharistic Prayer by praising God for giving us life, our beautiful universe, and the joy and love we share with one another.

Read this prayer slowly and then decorate it by drawing some of the things it mentions.

We thank you for all that is beautiful in the world
and for the happiness you have given us.
We praise you for daylight and for your word,
which lights up our minds.
We praise you for the earth,
for all the people who live on it,
and for our life, which comes from you.
We know that you are good.
You love us and do great things for us.

34

THEME: *The "Great Prayer"*

FOCUS: **The Liturgy of the Eucharist contains a great prayer of praise and thanksgiving.**

GOAL **To guide the children towards an attitude of thanksgiving as expressed in the "great prayer" of the Mass**

- Read paragraph one. Remind the children that there are several long prayers during this part of the Mass. Even if the children don't understand all of the words, or find it hard to pay attention, the important thing is that they understand that the words are expressing thanks and praise to God.
- Call attention to the illustrations on this page. Tell the children that these are just a few of the wonderful gifts God gives them. What catches their attention in particular?
- Read the next paragraph. Read each line of the prayer and have the children repeat it after you. You might even want to chant it (singing in a single note or tone) and have them chant it after you. Break the lines if they seem too long.
- Now ask the children to colour and illustrate the prayer (and add any gifts of nature for which they are grateful). They might want to add flowers, insects, trees, leaves, birds, fish, or lakes and rivers.

Did You Know?

Holy is the word that describes perfect goodness and love.

Glory is the praise we give to great beauty or majesty like God's.

Hosanna is a shout of joy from the Hebrew language.

Blessed means holy, great, and loved by God.

Do you sometimes give thanks to God during the day? For what are you most grateful? What words do you use?

Do you use your prayer corner sometimes? Remember, it is your very own space for praising and thanking God.

Let us Pray

Think about some of the wonderful things in your life. Then, with all your heart, mind, and voice, say this beautiful prayer of praise:

Holy, Holy,
Holy Lord God of hosts.
Heaven and earth
are full of your glory.
Hosanna
in the highest.

Blessed is he who comes
in the name of the Lord.
Hosanna
in the highest.

35

- Invite the children to answer each question in the middle of the left column. The focus is on the importance of private prayers of thanksgiving.
- The "Did You Know?" words are all ways of expressing praise and thanks to God. Go over the words and then have the children use them in prayers of their own. Here is an example:

Dear God, you are good and loving.
You are holy.
O God, glory be to you.
I praise you, God. Hosanna!
Dear God, you are great and holy.
Blessed are you!

- Tell the children that we say a "Let us Pray" prayer every Sunday at Mass. Have them think of some wonderful things in their lives. Then pray the prayer together and have the children take turns saying it. Point out that it uses the words they used above. Ask them to look for and circle the words *holy, glory, Hosanna,* and *blessed.* Ask which word is their favourite, and why.

Notes for Catechists

Your Own Prayer

At a meeting in 2009, Catholic bishops recommended that Catholic adults use a form of prayer called Lectio Divina, Latin for "divine reading," "spiritual reading," or "holy reading." This traditional Christian practice of prayer and scriptural reading draws us closer to God through Scripture. This is a way of praying with Scripture that invites us to study, ponder, listen, and commune with God.

Study: Read a Scripture passage slowly and attentively several times.

Ponder: Focus on something in the passage that caught your attention and quietly let it sink in.

Listen: Take time to open your heart and converse with God.

Commune: A simple, loving focus on God, resting in God's presence.

We Can Pray Always

At any moment in the day, somewhere in the world, Mass is being celebrated. The most beautiful prayer you can say any time of the day is a thanksgiving prayer, like the Eucharistic Prayer at Mass.

It only takes a minute and you will be together with Christians all over the world. Here is how you can do it.

1. Stretch your body until you feel relaxed.
2. Stand straight on both feet. Close your eyes. Remember that you are standing on our beautiful planet Earth!
3. Breathe deeply two or three times. Remember that God is looking at you with love.

Then pray this way:

Dear God, here I am,
giving thanks for this day.
With Jesus your Son,
I offer you praise.
I give you my love
and all that I do!
Amen.

MAY YOUR KINGDOM COME!

The Church Teaches...

It is always possible to pray. In fact, we NEED to pray.

- adapted for children from CCC #2757

THEME: We Can Pray Always

FOCUS: **We never pray alone; there are always people giving thanks in every land and language.**

GOAL **To help the children develop an attitude of prayerful thanksgiving as they learn about the Eucharistic Prayer**

- Read paragraphs one and two. Make the connection between the great thanksgiving prayer (the Eucharistic Prayer) at Mass and our own thanksgiving prayers.
- Draw attention to the children in the illustration. Tell the children in your group that you will be doing what the children in the illustration are doing. Now have them follow the directions by first stretching in silence a few times. Then ask them to stand straight on both feet and close their eyes. Then say: *You are standing right now on our beautiful planet Earth. Think about some of the things you love about Earth: the flowers, the trees, the ocean, the mountains, butterflies, animals, and birds.*
- Now read the final line, then have the children open their eyes and join in praying aloud and doing the gestures of the children in the illustrations, starting with "Dear God, here I am..." Do this slowly and reverently. End with the words "May your kingdom come!"
- Ask the children how they feel about this kind of prayer that involves their whole bodies. Encourage them to pray this way often, especially at home in their prayer corner.
- Share "The Church Teaches" and ask the children why they think we need to pray. Why is prayer a good thing to do? How do they feel when they pray?
- As the children leave, bless each one on the forehead saying, "_________, I thank God for you."

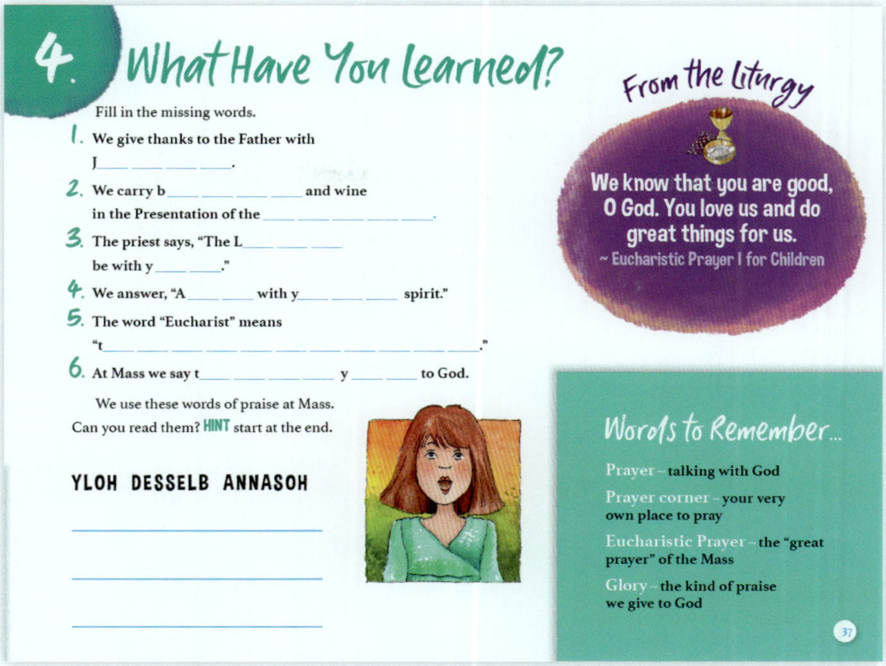

4. What Have You Learned?

Fill in the missing words.

1. We give thanks to the Father with J_ _ _ _ _.
2. We carry b_ _ _ _ _ and wine in the Presentation of the _ _ _ _ _ _.
3. The priest says, "The L_ _ _ _ be with y_ _ _."
4. We answer, "A_ _ _ with y_ _ _ _ spirit."
5. The word "Eucharist" means "t_ _ _ _ _ _ _ _ _ _ _ _ _ _ _."
6. At Mass we say t_ _ _ _ _ _ y_ _ _ to God.

We use these words of praise at Mass. Can you read them? **HINT** start at the end.

YLOH DESSELB ANNASOH

____

____

____

From the Liturgy

We know that you are good, O God. You love us and do great things for us.

~ Eucharistic Prayer I for Children

Words to Remember...

Prayer – talking with God

Prayer corner – your very own place to pray

Eucharistic Prayer – the "great prayer" of the Mass

Glory – the kind of praise we give to God

37

THEME: What Have You Learned?

FOCUS: We give thanks.

GOAL To help the children review what they have learned in Theme 4

- Go over the six sentences on the left and invite the children to give the correct answers. If no one can answer, encourage them to look back in their books. (*Answers are: Jesus, bread, Gifts, Lord, you, and, your, thanks, thank you.*) When all have completed the sentences, read them one by one and have the children repeat them after you. Then have six children read one each.
- Now go to the bottom left of the page and ask the children to unscramble the three words. Remind them that they studied these words on page 35.
- Review the "Words to Remember."
- Look together at the "From the Liturgy" prayer. Explain to the children that these words are used at Mass. Pray them dramatically and reverently.
- End by singing (to the tune of "The Farmer in the Dell"):

  We thank you, God, for Earth,
  we thank you, God, for Earth,
  Oh yes, we really do,
  we thank you, God, for Earth.

  Have the children suggest additional lines, such as We thank you, God, for trees; We thank you, God, for grass; We thank you, God, for sun; and so on.

5. We Remember and Celebrate

Most of us like to remember and celebrate the important days in our lives.

On the day of your First Communion, your family will remember the great joy they felt when you were born. They want this day to be very special for you and they will celebrate it with you.

At Mass we celebrate Jesus! We remember his last meal, his death, and his resurrection. We remember that he loved and served others.

We remember that he promised to be with us always.

THEME: *We Remember and Celebrate*

FOCUS: **The key moments in life are worth celebrating and celebrating well.**

GOAL **To introduce the children to the Eucharistic Prayer, the great prayer of thanksgiving at Mass**

- Read the first sentence. Remind the children that one of the most important days in their lives is coming soon. Then read the second paragraph. Do they know yet how they and their families will celebrate this day? What will be the most important moment of it? Who else will be there with them? What are they looking forward to the most? The children will likely focus on externals (such as what they will wear or what they will eat at the party afterwards), so after this sharing, remind them that on this important day they will be receiving Jesus for the first time at Mass.
- Have them focus on the illustration and ask them to identify the objects (symbols). What do they know about bread, wine, grapes? Why are there balloons, streamers, and other decorations?

A Prayer for You

Dear God, as I move with these children
towards the experience of communion with Jesus,
open my mind and heart to your light.
Help me to find the words to welcome them
into your loving embrace.
Help me to convey an attitude of joy
and a desire for your peace in their hearts.
Guide me, loving God,
as I guide these children
towards their First Holy Communion.
Amen.

At Mass, the priest repeats the words of Jesus from the Last Supper. He takes the bread in his hands and says, as Jesus said:

Take this, all of you, and eat of it, for this is my Body, which will be given up for you.

Then the priest takes the cup of wine and says, as Jesus said:

Take this, all of you, and drink from it, for this is the chalice of my Blood.

After each of these invitations, the priest shows us the bread, then the wine, which have become the presence of the risen Jesus among us.

39

- Read the third paragraph on page 38. Ask: What does it mean to remember? How did Jesus love and serve others? What did Jesus promise us? How is Jesus with us? Allow time for the children to share their answers, then read the last sentence on page 38. (Note: *There is no one correct way to answer, so listen carefully to what children are saying. This is a good way to learn if they are on track or totally off the mark in their understanding*.)
- Together look at page 39. Ask the children to describe the illustrations. What is Jesus doing? What is the priest doing?
- Now read the text at the top left, including these words: “Take this, all of you, and eat of it, for this is my Body, which will be given up for you.” Explain that at the Last Supper, Jesus was asking his followers to stay close to him—so close that he could live in their hearts. When they shared the bread, they were saying “Yes” to Jesus and his teachings. They were opening their hearts to Jesus completely.
- Now read the text at the top right, including these words: “Take this, all of you, and drink from it, for this is the chalice of my Blood.” Explain that by giving his followers his body and blood, Jesus was giving them his very life. He was giving himself to be with them always. At every Mass, we remember this, and we accept Jesus and his teachings again each time we receive communion.
- Read the final paragraph. Do the children remember seeing the priest hold up the bread and then the cup? (In some parishes, bells are rung at these two moments to signal their importance.)

From the Bible

Jesus told his friends, "When two or three of you are together in my name, I am with you."
~ adapted from Matthew 18:20

We "See" with Faith

At the Last Supper, the apostles saw Jesus with their own eyes. At Mass we do not see him. But we believe that he is with us. That is why the priest invites us to proclaim our faith.

The priest says:

The mystery of faith.

All reply with great joy:

We proclaim your Death, O Lord, and profess your Resurrection until you come again.

The Church Teaches...

Jesus himself is with us, though we can't see him, at every Eucharistic celebration.
- adapted for children from CCC #1348

40

Can you finish these sentences?

- Jesus died on the C____ ____ ____ ____.
- God r____ ____ ____ ____ ____ Jesus from the dead.
- J____ ____ ____ ____ will come again.

THEME: We "See" with Faith

FOCUS: **Jesus is not physically present to us, yet he is with us. This is the mystery of faith.**

GOAL To emphasize for the children the spiritual presence of Jesus in the Eucharistic liturgy

- Share the "From the Bible" words and discuss them. What do the children think these words mean? Share what you think they mean. Explain that gathering in Jesus' name is different from gathering in a playground or classroom at school. We gather in his name when we come together to pray; when we say grace around the family table; and especially when we come to the Lord's Supper.
- Read the first paragraph. Some children at this age may think that the priest is Jesus, and they *can* see the priest. Explain that Jesus promised to be with us in many ways, but above all in the bread and wine that become his body and blood. We see the bread and wine, but we do not see Jesus himself. Yet we believe he is with us, and so the priest invites us to express this. Proclaim as the priest does: "The mystery of faith." Practise the response several times, with the children repeating it after you. Then have each one read it (with great joy!).
- Ask the children to focus on the illustration. What do they see? Why is the cross full of light? What good things does it represent? Invite them to draw their own cross and decorate it with happy colours and objects. They can place these in their prayer corner at home.
- Go over the three sentences at the bottom right. Explain that we "proclaim" these three things every Sunday at Mass: Jesus died for us; he was raised from the dead; and he will come again.
- Ask the children to look at "The Church Teaches." This is one of the key teachings of our Catholic faith, as noted above. Explain that "Eucharistic celebration" is another way to say "Mass."

We Imitate Jesus

After giving them the bread and the wine, Jesus told his friends: "Do this in memory of me." At Mass we celebrate in memory of him. But remembering Jesus also means following him on the path to God's love.

When we do something that is difficult for us, we call it a **sacrifice.** And when we sacrifice for someone else, we are following Jesus.

Can you remember a sacrifice you made for someone? In the frame on this page, draw a picture of what you did.

41

THEME: ## We Imitate Jesus

FOCUS: Following Jesus on the path of God's love ultimately involves sacrifice.

GOAL **To introduce the idea of sacrifice at a level children can understand**

- Read the first paragraph. Then ask: After he gave them the bread and wine, what did Jesus say to his friends? What does it mean to do something "in memory" of someone? If your grandparents live far away, how do you remember them? If one of your grandparents has died, how do you remember him or her? Do you remember God's Law of Love? What is it? ("You shall love the Lord your God with all your heart, and with all your soul, and with all your mind... and you shall love your neighbour as yourself." [Matthew 22:34-39]) Is it difficult to follow Jesus on the path to God's love? Why or why not?
- Explain that when we do something difficult for others, the action is called a sacrifice. This is what Jesus did. His whole life was dedicated to living God's Law of Love. When those in charge wanted him to act another way, he refused. They arrested Jesus and killed him because he did not obey their law, but obeyed only God's Law of Love. Jesus gave his life rather than turn away from God's law. This is the greatest sacrifice, to give one's life for another person.
- Ask a child to read the next two paragraphs. If the children can't remember a sacrifice they have made, perhaps they can write about someone else's sacrifice: a soldier in the war; a parent who gives up certain things so his or her children can have food and shelter; a firefighter or police officer who risks his or her life for others; etc. Or, if they prefer, they can write a note to Jesus thanking him for following God's Law of Love, even to death.
- Have the children look at the two frames. What do they say? Explain that when we come together at Mass (Eucharist), we remember the sacrifice Jesus made for us.

THEME: *Alex Makes a Sacrifice*

FOCUS: The greatest of all sacrifices is to give one's life for another.

GOAL To give the children a practical example of a sacrifice

- Read the first two paragraphs, then have the children follow the illustrated dialogue on pages 42 and 43. Invite them to take the various parts: Sam, Alex, Alex's mother, Sam's mother. Once they have read through the dialogue, ask: How did Sam feel about being sick? Where was Alex first invited? What did Sam's mother call to ask Alex's mother? How did Alex feel about the two invitations? Which one do you think he wanted to accept?

Notes for Catechists

Going to Mass

What do you do about children who do not go to Mass and are preparing for First Communion? Start by telling parents that celebrating Sunday liturgy is an essential part of preparing for First Communion. Invite them to call you to talk about this, or, if you can arrange it with your parish priest or faith formation director, parents can call him or her. In class, invite the children to come to Mass with their parents to celebrate, greet others, sing, pray, and remember Jesus. Have them make invitations for their parents that say: "You are invited to Sunday Mass. Love, Jesus." Be open and inviting and welcoming, and pray for the children and their parents. If your parish or diocese has regulations about preparing children who do not belong to a particular parish, be sure to check and observe these.

From the Bible

"People will know you are my followers when you show love for one another."
~ adapted from John 13:35

What Do You Think?

- What was Alex's sacrifice?
- Do you think it was difficult for Alex to give up going skating?
- Why do you think Alex did it?

43

- Continue to question: What did Alex decide? What did Alex do then? How did Sam feel about Alex's decision? Once the children have discussed the situation, invite them to role-play it, adding their own dialogue if they wish.
- Go over the "What Do You Think?" questions. Give the children time to answer and discuss. If necessary, help them fill in their answers on page 43. Then ask: Have you ever given up something you wanted to help someone else?
  Explain that we are showing love for others when we sacrifice for them. That is what Jesus did. He loved us so much that he gave up his life to show us how to follow God's path.
- Proclaim the "From the Bible" words, loudly and clearly. Ask: Who is saying these words? Who do we Christians follow? Now have the children read the statement together.
- Look at the following "Did You Know?" statements. Read the first one. Then ask the class, "Did *you* know this?" in an exaggerated manner (as if you are astonished). Then read the second statement, and so on, each time asking, "Did *you* know this?" When all the statements are read, ask: "Where did you learn so much?" Invite the children to comment.

Did You Know?

Liturgical Words

Liturgy is the public prayer of the Church.
Eucharist is a Greek word that means "thanksgiving." Giving thanks is at the heart of the liturgy.
The **Liturgy of the Eucharist** is the part of the Mass when the gifts are prepared and the presider (priest) proclaims the Eucharistic Prayer.
The **Eucharistic Prayer** is a prayer of thanksgiving and the high point of the entire celebration of the Mass.
The **Breaking of the Bread** is the moment when the presider (priest) recreates gestures of Christ at the Last Supper. The action signifies that "in communion," we who are many are made one in the one Bread of Life, which is Christ.
Amen is a Hebrew word meaning "It is true." In the Great Amen, we say that we believe all that has been said and done in the Eucharistic Prayer.

We Pray Together

Every week at Mass, we celebrate with others in our parish because Jesus is with us. We sing together, pray together, and share the Lord's Supper. We need one another. Together we try to follow the path to God.

During the Eucharistic Prayer, we pray for one another and for people all over the world. Here's what the priest says in our name:

Father, because you love us, you invite us to come to your table. Fill us with the joy of the Holy Spirit as we receive the body and blood of your Son.

Lord, you never forget any of your children. We ask you to take care of those we love, especially of ____________ and ____________, and we pray for those who have died. Remember everyone who is suffering from pain or sorrow.

Remember Christians everywhere and all other people in the world.

We are filled with wonder and praise when we see what you do for us through Jesus your Son.

~ Eucharistic Prayer I for Children

44

THEME: We Pray Together

FOCUS: **The Eucharistic liturgy reminds us to pray for our brothers and sisters all over the world.**

GOAL **To highlight that the Eucharistic Prayer is also for others, in heaven and on earth**

- Invite the children to look at the photograph. What do they see? How does the priest look? What is he doing?
- Read paragraph one. Explain to the children that we are "in communion" with all those who believe in Jesus. We are "in communion" with all the people in our parish. At Mass, we are also in communion with Jesus, in whose name we gather.
- Read paragraph two. Then have different children take turns reading the prayer the priest says, line by line. You read the line that begins with "We ask you to take care ...." When you get to the first blank, fill in the names of half the children; fill in the other half at the second blank.
- Then let the children continue.
- At the end of the prayer, ask: What does God invite us to do? What do we ask to be filled with? Does God ever forget us? Who are some of the people we remember? Do you know anyone who is sick or injured right now? Why are we filled with wonder and praise?
- Invite each child to take a turn reading the lines you read earlier and filling in the two blanks with the names of people they want to remember in prayer.

- Read paragraph one. Allow time for the children to answer and comment. Ask if they know anyone who has died. Remind them that at every Mass, the priest, in our name, prays for our loved ones who have died.
- Ask a child to read the second paragraph. Do they know what the Church calls people who are in heaven? (*saints*) Who else lives in heaven? (*God, Jesus, Holy Spirit, Mary, the angels*) Explain to the children that we can pray to the saints in heaven and they can pray for us. We can also pray to angels. Share this Guardian Angel prayer with them:

  Angel of God, my guardian dear,
  to whom God's love commits me here,
  ever this day be at my side,
  to light, to guard, to rule, and guide. Amen.

  Ask the children to close their eyes and repeat the words after you. Explain that angels are God's messengers. They watch over us, just as the saints do.
- Now read the prayer after "At Mass we pray." Ask: Where do we ask to gather? How will we feel in God's kingdom? Who will be there with us? Who are the friends of Jesus? What will these friends do together?
- Ask the children to look at the illustration and to comment on it. Who is pictured? How do they look? Are they happy or sad? What do they like best about the picture?

We Offer Ourselves

We began the great prayer of the Eucharist by offering bread and wine to God. Through the Holy Spirit, these gifts became the presence of the risen Lord.

Now, at the end of this great prayer, we offer *ourselves* with Jesus. The priest prays:

Through him, and with him, and in him,
O God, almighty Father,
in the unity of the Holy Spirit,
all glory and honour is yours, for ever and ever.

All sing the great Amen.

Amen!
Amen, yes, I believe,
Amen, Amen, Amen!

Every person gathered at Mass is saying yes to Jesus. Yes, Jesus, we believe you are here with us. Yes, we want to be one with you.

When you sing the great Amen, what is in your mind and heart?

Write your thoughts in the empty bubble in the picture on this page.

46

THEME: *We Offer Ourselves*

FOCUS: **When we say "Amen" at Mass, we are saying "yes" to all that Jesus teaches.**

GOAL **To help children deepen their understanding of saying "yes" to Jesus at Mass and in their lives**

- Ask one of the children to read paragraph one. Explain that now we are at the end of the great prayer of thanksgiving and it is time to offer ourselves to God with Jesus.
- Read paragraph two. Line by line, proclaim what the priest prays and have the children repeat after you with arms uplifted. The priest will sometimes chant this closing prayer. Feel free to chant it for the children (a one-tone, one-note prayer) and have them repeat after you.
- If you know the "Amen" sung in your parish, review it now with the children. Otherwise, simply chant it three times. Ask: What does "Amen" mean?
- Have a child read the four lines that follow the prayer. Explain that the Amen we sing or say at this time in the Mass is called the Great Amen because it follows the great prayer of thanksgiving we have just prayed.
- Ask the children to focus on the illustration. Who do they see? How do the people look? Now read the last two paragraphs and have the children put their own words in the bubble.

Notes for Catechists

When We Say "Amen"

Catholics believe that Jesus is present in the Eucharist and that he offers his body and blood as food and drink so that we might be made holy. This is one of the great mysteries of our faith. We can't see a change in the bread or wine, but we believe in it. We can't see Jesus, but we believe he is present. When we say "Amen" or "Yes" to this great mystery, we are saying yes to all of it: to everything Jesus taught and to his way of life.

5. What Have You Learned?

Try to match these two columns. Draw a line to the correct answer.

1. The last meal of Jesus	a. The great prayer of thanksgiving
2. Presentation of the Gifts	b. We say yes to our faith
3. Offertory collection (part of the Preparation of the Gifts)	c. We give some of our own money
4. Sacrifice	d. The Last Supper
5. Eucharistic Prayer	e. We carry the bread and wine
6. Great Amen	f. We give up something we like for someone

Spend time at prayer thinking about Jesus and how he is always with you. At Mass, this is what we remember and celebrate. Here is how you can talk to Jesus about this:

1. Sit down in your special prayer corner.
2. Close your eyes.
3. Breathe slowly and deeply a few times until you feel quiet inside.
4. In a very soft voice or in your heart, slowly say a short prayer from the Mass: for example, "Holy, holy, holy" or "Blessed are you" or "Amen."
5. Say it over and over, as often as you like, until the peace of God fills your heart.
6. Now share with Jesus whatever is in your heart.
7. End your prayer time with these words: "Through Jesus, all glory and honour is yours, almighty Father, for ever and ever. Amen."

From the Bible

"My father and I will come to you and make our home with you."
~ adapted from John 14:23

47

THEME: *What Have You Learned?*

FOCUS: We remember and celebrate.

GOAL To help the children review what they have learned in Theme 5

- Help the children to match the columns. If they have forgotten what a word or phrase means, review these with them.
- Remind the children that Jesus is always with them: this is what they remember and celebrate at Mass. But they can talk to Jesus anytime, anywhere—especially at home in their prayer corner. Now lead them through the prayer experience one step at a time. Allow enough time for each step. Invite them to discuss this experience if they wish.
- Share the "From the Bible" words. Ask: Who said these words? (*Jesus*) What do you think they mean? (*God is with us always*) Where can God make a home in us? (*in our hearts, our inner selves*) Now invite each child to proclaim these words of Jesus in a loud, clear voice.
- Before the children leave, sign each with a cross on the forehead, saying, "May God be in your heart this day." The children answer, "Amen."

Notes for Catechists

Communicate with Parents

At this point in the preparation process, you might want to send a note home to parents, reminding them to help their child review the various parts of the Mass, as described in the child's book. They might also pay close attention to how attentive their child is during Mass, making sure to bring their attention back to what is happening. Also ask parents to go over the Our Father, Hail Mary, Glory to God, and Sign of the Cross, and any other prayers they pray as a family. If you have information about the date and time for the sacrament or any other information parents might need or appreciate, share it in this note as well.

6. We Share the Bread of Life

Very soon you will celebrate your First Communion! The word **communion** means "being together," but it means even more than that. It means "being together in love."

When we share the Bread of Life, we are in communion with Jesus.

Did You Know?

- **We can be in communion with those around us.**
- **We can be in communion in spirit, as we are with Jesus.**
- **We can be in communion even with someone who is far away from us.**

Trinh's mother was going to London on a business trip. She was going to be gone for a week. Trinh didn't want her mother to miss her. When her mom was not looking, Trinh put a picture of herself in her mom's suitcase.

THEME: We Share the Bread of Life

FOCUS: **We remember Jesus, we celebrate Jesus, we believe that Jesus is present.**

GOAL **To introduce the children to the concept of being "in communion"**

- Read the first two paragraphs. "Communion" is not a common word for many children. They may have heard and used the word "community," but "communion" is by and large a Church word, as in "receiving communion." Take time, therefore, to explain what being "in communion" with someone means. When we receive Jesus in communion, we are together with him in love. In other words, when we say "Amen" to receiving Jesus, we are saying "Amen" to God's Law of Love. This "Amen" affects our lives day in and day out, not just on Sunday or at the moment of receiving Jesus in the Eucharist.
- Go over the "Did You Know?" statements. Read the first one and ask the children if they understand it. How can they be in communion with one another? (*by hearing the same lessons, by working together, by believing in Jesus, etc.*)
- Read statement two. Explain that the words "in spirit" apply when someone is not physically present. This can be a parent who is out of town, a family member or friend who has died, the angels and saints, and Jesus himself. One of the best ways to be in communion with Jesus is through holy communion: the children will experience this at their First Communion and every time they receive communion. Other ways to be in communion with Jesus are through prayer, following his teaching, and living God's Law of Love.
- Read statement three. Explain that the following story shows one way to be in communion with someone who is far away from us.

When Trinh's mother arrived at her hotel room, she opened her suitcase. She found Trinh's picture and put it on the table next to her bed. She was so happy to see Trinh's smiling face there beside her.

Trinh understood that even though her mother was travelling, they still could be together. They still could be "in communion."

When people really love and understand one another as Trinh and her mother do, they are in communion. When they share hopes and dreams and work together, they are in communion.

From the Liturgy

Send the Holy Spirit to all of us who share in this meal. May this Spirit bring us closer together in the family of the Church.
~ Eucharistic Prayer II for Children

49

- Share the story of Trinh and her mother on pages 48 and 49. Ask: Does your mother or father travel often? How do you keep in touch (in communion) when he or she is gone? How did Trinh and her mother stay in communion with each other?
- Proclaim the "From the Liturgy" words yourself, then have the children repeat them after you line by line. Ask: What "meal" is this prayer referring to? What is another word for "bringing us closer"? (*communion*) What is the family of the Church? (*all Catholics, my parish*)

Did You Know?

The Holy Spirit

It is difficult for adults, and even more difficult for children, to understand the concept of three persons in one God. If the children raise this question, you might use the following information.

The Holy Spirit is one of the three persons in God: Father, Son, and Holy Spirit. The Bible teaches that there is only one living God, yet we learn from Scripture that God is Father, Son, and Holy Spirit. One way to partially visualize this idea is to think of water. Water is a single compound that can exist in three states: liquid, ice, and vapour. An egg is another example. It is comprised of the white, the yoke, and the shell, yet it is still one egg. St. Patrick used a three-leaf clover to illustrate that there is one stem but three leaves on it. Of course, these examples do not begin to paint a complete picture of our God, but they do show that the three "persons" in no way invalidate God's oneness. The Blessed Trinity—God the Father, the Son, and the Holy Spirit—is one of the great mysteries of our faith and can never be fully explained in human terms.

We Celebrate Sacraments

The Church has very special celebrations called **sacraments** that keep us in communion with God and one another. The sacraments are signs of love from Jesus.

Can you fill in the names of these sacraments?

In b________________, Jesus tells us through the sign of water: **"God my Father loves you. You are God's own child."**

In H____________ C________________, Jesus tells us through the signs of bread and wine: **"I am the Living Bread. Whoever eats this bread will have life forever."**

By calling us God's children in baptism and giving himself to us in Communion, Jesus is saying, "I am with you always."

THEME: We Celebrate Sacraments

FOCUS: **The sacraments of initiation are baptism, Eucharist, and confirmation.**

GOAL **To remind the children that the sacraments keep us "in communion" as believers**

- Invite the children to focus on the photograph on the left. What do they see? What is this ceremony called? Have they ever been to a baptism? What do they remember about it?
- What does the photograph on the right show? What is happening? What is the child doing?
- Read paragraph one. Explain that there are seven signs of love from Jesus, but here we are looking at two of the first sacraments we celebrate: Baptism and Eucharist or Holy Communion. Invite them to fill in the names of these two sacraments. (Help with the spelling if they need you.) Ask: Which sacrament uses water? Which uses bread and wine? What does Jesus tell us in baptism? (Have the children read together, "God my Father ....") What does Jesus tell us through Holy Communion? (Have the children read together, "I am the Living Bread ....") Now invite each child to choose one of these messages from Jesus and proclaim it loudly and clearly. When all have had a turn, read the final paragraph. Ask: What is Jesus saying to you in *both* these sacraments?
- Invite the children to write out and decorate these words of Jesus: "I am with you always." They can take these pages home for their prayer corner.

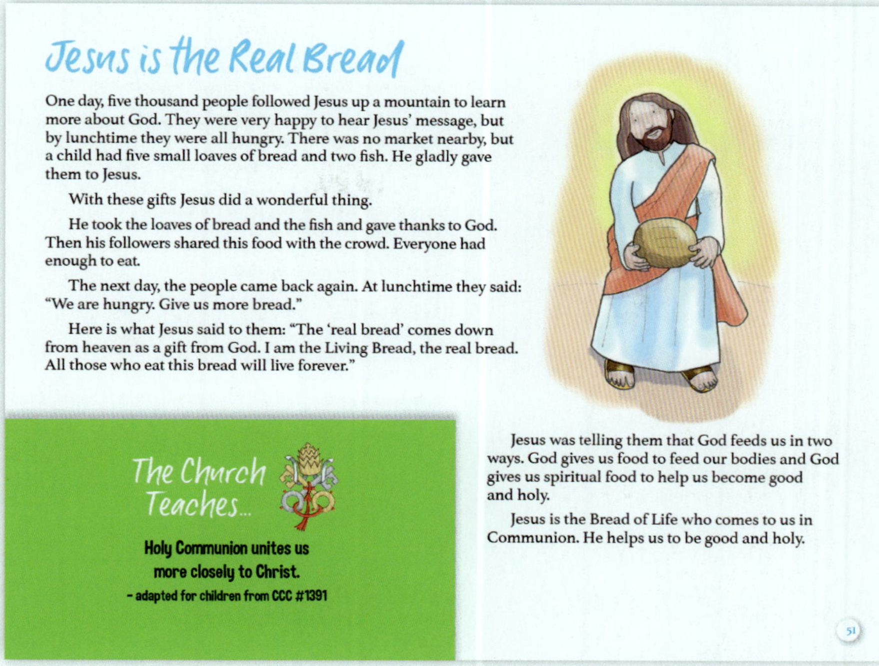

Jesus is the Real Bread

One day, five thousand people followed Jesus up a mountain to learn more about God. They were very happy to hear Jesus' message, but by lunchtime they were all hungry. There was no market nearby, but a child had five small loaves of bread and two fish. He gladly gave them to Jesus.

With these gifts Jesus did a wonderful thing.

He took the loaves of bread and the fish and gave thanks to God. Then his followers shared this food with the crowd. Everyone had enough to eat.

The next day, the people came back again. At lunchtime they said: "We are hungry. Give us more bread."

Here is what Jesus said to them: "The 'real bread' comes down from heaven as a gift from God. I am the Living Bread, the real bread. All those who eat this bread will live forever."

The Church Teaches...

Holy Communion unites us more closely to Christ.

– adapted for children from CCC #1391

Jesus was telling them that God feeds us in two ways. God gives us food to feed our bodies and God gives us spiritual food to help us become good and holy.

Jesus is the Bread of Life who comes to us in Communion. He helps us to be good and holy.

51

THEME: Jesus Is the Real Bread

FOCUS: **Jesus feeds hungry hearts, and we are called to do the same.**

GOAL **To share the loaves and fishes story, as well as the concept of Jesus as living bread, with the children**

- Read over the first three paragraphs yourself so you can "tell" the story rather than reading it to the children. Ask them to picture this scene, to imagine all those people and only five small loaves of bread and two small fish. The child gladly shared this food with Jesus, and Jesus shared it with the whole crowd. How did he do this?
- Invite the children to look at the illustration on the right. What is Jesus doing? (*point them to paragraph three*) After Jesus gave thanks, what happened?
- Read the next two paragraphs. The people came back, but what did they want? What do the children think Jesus meant when he said he was the "real bread," the "living bread"? (The important point here is that Jesus was making a distinction between the bread we eat for physical sustenance and the bread that feeds our spirit. In communion, he feeds our spirit.)
- Ask a child to read the final two paragraphs. Emphasize that in communion, Jesus feeds our spirit (our soul) to help us become good and holy, to help us live God's Law of Love. Communion is not meant to feed us physically.
- Share "The Church Teaches." Proclaim it and have the children repeat it after you five times.

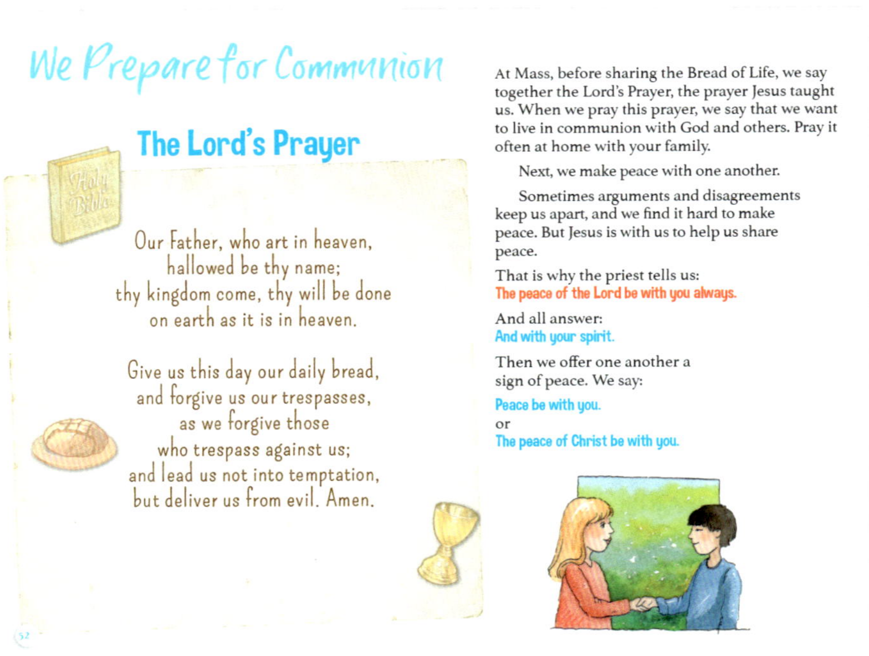

We Prepare for Communion

The Lord's Prayer

Our Father, who art in heaven,
hallowed be thy name;
thy kingdom come, thy will be done
on earth as it is in heaven.

Give us this day our daily bread,
and forgive us our trespasses,
as we forgive those
who trespass against us;
and lead us not into temptation,
but deliver us from evil. Amen.

At Mass, before sharing the Bread of Life, we say together the Lord's Prayer, the prayer Jesus taught us. When we pray this prayer, we say that we want to live in communion with God and others. Pray it often at home with your family.

Next, we make peace with one another.

Sometimes arguments and disagreements keep us apart, and we find it hard to make peace. But Jesus is with us to help us share peace.

That is why the priest tells us:
The peace of the Lord be with you always.

And all answer:
And with your spirit.

Then we offer one another a sign of peace. We say:

Peace be with you.
or
The peace of Christ be with you.

THEME: *We Prepare for Communion*

FOCUS: **Your kingdom come; your will be done.**

GOAL **To walk the children through the communion rite**

- Read the first paragraph and then focus on the Our Father (The Lord's Prayer). Children should know this prayer by heart, but if they don't, read it line by line, with them repeating it after you. Then assign nine children to proclaim one line each. As they do this, have them open the palms of their hands with arms slightly raised. This is the gesture recommended by the Roman Missal (the official guide to the prayers and gestures of the liturgy). Encourage the children to do this at Mass when they pray the Our Father.
- Have the children look at the illustration at the bottom. Ask: What are the children doing? Do you remember sharing peace at Mass? Explain that it is more than shaking hands with people. This is truly meant to be a time to exchange the peace of Christ.
- Now have the children take turns reading the remaining paragraphs. Invite each to take a turn being the priest, with all answering, "And with your spirit." When all have had a turn, ask the children to offer one another and you a sign of peace using these words: "The peace of Christ be with you." ("Christ" is Jesus. This is not his last name, but rather a title given to him by others. It means "messiah" or "saviour.")

We Ask for Mercy

Maybe there is someone you would like to make peace with, but this person is not present. Maybe you never had the chance to say "sorry."

This point in the Mass is a time to ask God to forgive us for anything we forgot about. We can ask for forgiveness for anything we may have done to hurt others.

Lamb of God, you take away the sins of the world,
have mercy on us.

Lamb of God, you take away the sins of the world,
have mercy on us.

Lamb of God, you take away the sins of the world,
grant us peace.

Lamb of God is one of the special names the Church uses for Jesus.

53

THEME: We Ask for Mercy

FOCUS: **In the Eucharistic liturgy, Jesus, the Lamb of God, forgives us and shares God's peace with us.**

GOAL **To acquaint children with the title "Lamb of God" and to share the meaning of the "Lamb of God" prayer at Mass**

- Read the first paragraph. What and who do they see in the photographs? What is going on? Now invite them to close their eyes and think of someone to whom they might want to say "sorry." Tell them to picture this person and picture themselves talking over the problem they have. Ask them to say "sorry" in their hearts. (Tell them to be sure to apologize in person the first chance they get.) Now ask them to think of anything else they are sorry about and to tell this to God in their own words. Explain that this is what we do at Mass before we receive Jesus in communion.
- Read paragraph two.
- Have the children take turns being the priest. First, review what the priest says to the people at Mass, and their response. Explain that "Lamb of God" is a name for Jesus. "Have mercy on us" means "please forgive us."

Notes for Catechists

The Paschal Lamb

A lamb is a symbol of Easter because Christians view Jesus Christ as "the Lamb of God," sacrificed for the sins of the world. This lamb, known as the Paschal lamb, was borrowed from the Jewish feast of Passover. For Jews, the lamb of Passover was sacrificed and its blood was placed on the doorposts of the Hebrew slaves' homes. The angel of death then passed over these homes before the Exodus (Exodus 12:1-30). Early Christians saw that the Lord himself was the Passover or Paschal lamb. In the person of Jesus, Christians experience new life and promise!

We Are One with Jesus

Now comes the great moment you are preparing for. The people go towards the altar to receive Holy Communion. Soon you will be able to do this, too.

The priest holds up the bread and says: **The Body of Christ.**

The people bow slightly and put forward their cupped hands. As they receive the host in their hand, each person answers: **Amen.**

Then they put the host in their mouth.

The priest might also offer the wine, saying: **The Blood of Christ.**

People bow slightly and reach for the chalice. Each answers: **Amen.**

Then they take a sip from the cup.

Now the Mass is drawing to a close.

The priest or deacon turns to the people and says:

Go forth, the Mass is ended.

All answer: **Thanks be to God!**

Remember, when you leave the church, Jesus goes with you. He walks with you always in all that you do.

THEME: *We Are One with Jesus*

FOCUS: **We are going to meet our great friend, the Lord Jesus himself.**

GOAL **To teach the children how to approach and receive communion**

- Read the first paragraph, then ask the children how they feel about their approaching First Communion. What do they think is most important about this day? What are they most looking forward to? Allow time for them to share their feelings.
- Now review the words and gestures they will use when receiving Jesus for the first time. Read the next three paragraphs. Have the children form a line and practise coming forward (with you as priest or communion minister), bowing slightly and holding out their hands, palms up, with the right hand on top of the left. After you mime handing them a host or piece of unleavened bread, say, "The Body of Christ." They say, "Amen," loudly and clearly. Practise until everyone gets it right.

  (Note: *It is not in the communion rite to make the Sign of the Cross after receiving the Body of Christ, yet this seems to be a local custom in many parishes.*)
- Read the next four paragraphs, then practise with the chalice. (Use a cup of grape juice, but first check to be sure no children have allergy issues.) Again have the children form a line and come forward. You offer the cup, saying, "The Blood of Christ." With a slight bow, they take the cup and say, "Amen," loudly and clearly. Be sure they know to take a sip, not a gulp. Practise until every child gets it right.
- Ask the children to look at the photograph on page 54 and to comment on it. Point out that they are to be respectful and quiet as they approach the table of the Lord. What they wear is not as important as how they feel in their hearts. This is a great moment, a time of joy and peace.
- Explain that when the priest puts the hosts that are not used back in the tabernacle (the gold container in which consecrated hosts are kept) after communion, all sit quietly for a few moments and speak to Jesus in their hearts. Invite the children to share what they might want to say to Jesus at that time. Now read what the priest or deacon says to the people. Have the children take turns being the presider: all answer, "Thanks be to God" in loud, clear voices.

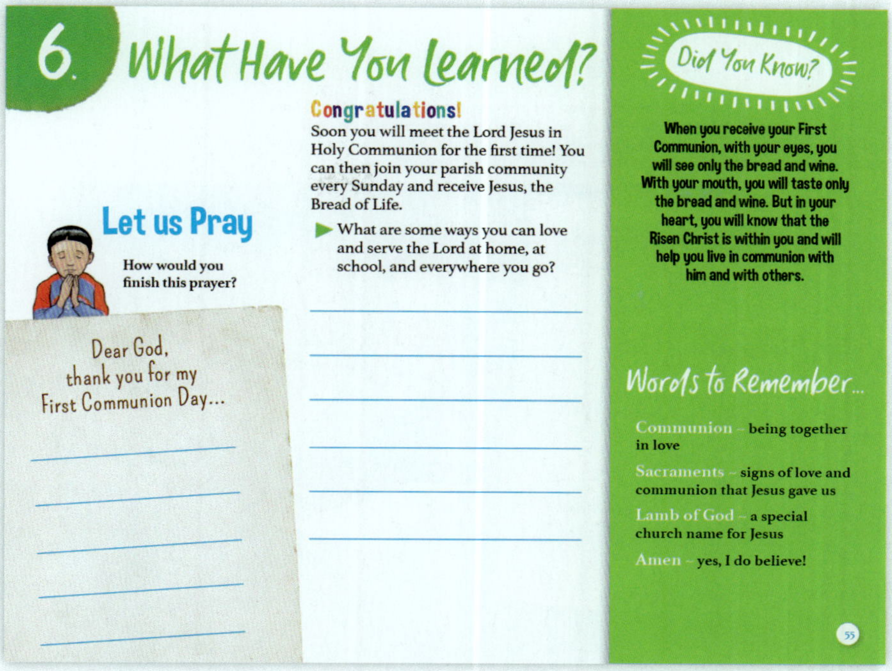

6. What Have You Learned?

Congratulations!

Soon you will meet the Lord Jesus in Holy Communion for the first time! You can then join your parish community every Sunday and receive Jesus, the Bread of Life.

▶ What are some ways you can love and serve the Lord at home, at school, and everywhere you go?

Let us Pray

How would you finish this prayer?

Dear God,
thank you for my
First Communion Day...

Did You Know?

When you receive your First Communion, with your eyes, you will see only the bread and wine. With your mouth, you will taste only the bread and wine. But in your heart, you will know that the Risen Christ is within you and will help you live in communion with him and with others.

Words to Remember...

Communion – being together in love

Sacraments – signs of love and communion that Jesus gave us

Lamb of God – a special church name for Jesus

Amen – yes, I do believe!

55

Theme: What Have You Learned?

FOCUS: We share the Bread of Life.

GOAL To review what the children have learned in Theme 6

- Go over the "Words to Remember" and be sure the children can explain them in their own words. Ask: Which sacrament(s) have you already received? Which sacrament will you soon be celebrating? Who is the Lamb of God? What are some things we say "Amen" to?
- Now review together the "Did You Know?" statement.
- Ask the children to complete the sentence in the "Let us Pray" section at the bottom of page 55. Let them share their answers and then offer your own explanation.
- Invite them to answer the question in the middle of the page and share their responses with others, if they choose.

Prayers to Remember

In this book you have learned about the Mass and the prayers we pray at Mass. You will find some of these prayers in *My Prayer Book*, which your parent or teacher can print for you.* You might want to learn some of these prayers by heart. Pray them at home in your prayer corner. Pray them joyfully at Mass. Pray them every day wherever you are!

How to make your very own prayer book

You will need:
- scissors
- ribbon, string, wool, or staples to hold your book together
- a marker or coloured pencil

To make your prayer book:
- Cut out the pages of *My Prayer Book* with scissors.
- Fold each page in half.
- Use ribbon, string, wool, or staples to hold your book together.
- Write your name in marker or coloured pencil in your prayer book.

* Parents and catechists: My Prayer Book is available for download and printing at en.novalis.ca/my-prayer-book/

56

Prayers to Remember

Making their very own prayer books to take home and keep is a fun activity for the children. Gather the materials they will need and let their creativity flow! (Order extra activities for children free of charge at **twentythirdpublications.com** in the FREE E-Resources section.) When the books are finished, invite the children to show each other their books.

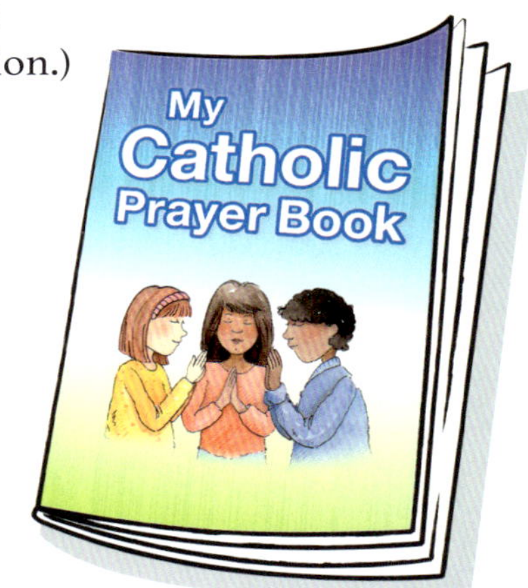

Then ask volunteers to take turns leading a prayer. Others can read along silently or aloud.

Remind the children that these are prayers they can pray anytime and anywhere. Encourage them to keep their prayer books in a handy place at home so they can learn all the prayers by heart.

Parents and catechists: *My Catholic Prayer Book* is available for free at **twentythirdpublications.com** in the FREE E-Resources section

Thank you...

... for a job well done! You have been an important guide and mentor as the children in your care prepared for their First Communion. Your dedication and your willingness to share your faith are a great gift to the children, their families, and your parish.

We hope that you have grown in your faith and your understanding of Eucharist through this rich experience. May your relationship with Jesus continue to nourish and strengthen you in all you do!

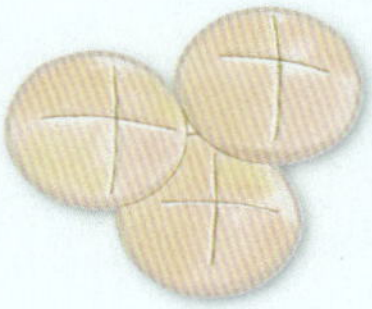

Suggestions for Your Bookshelf

Celebrating Eucharist: A Mass Book for Children. New London, CT: Twenty-Third Publications, 2011.

Clark, Connie. *My First Communion Activity Book*. New London, CT: Twenty-Third Publications, 2014.

Clark, Connie. *My First Reconciliation Activity Book*. New London, CT: Twenty-Third Publications, 2014.

Hope Dawson, Glynnis, and John Dawson. *Guided Meditations for Catholic Kids*. Toronto, Canada: Novalis, 2018.

Lepine, Michelle. *21 Activities that Really Work*. Toronto, Canada: Novalis, 2017.

Murphy, Doris. *Learning Centers for First Reconciliation, First Eucharist, and the Whole Community*. New London, CT: Twenty-Third Publications, 2007.

Way Skinner, Christine, illustrated by Céleste Gagnon. *We Go to Mass*. Toronto, Canada: Novalis, 2017.

Way Skinner, Christine, illustrated by Céleste Gagnon. *We Pray in Many Ways*. Toronto, Canada: Novalis, 2017.

Faith Facts

What the Priest Wears at Mass

Alb: An ankle-length white linen vestment with sleeves. (The alb is a sign of baptism, which is why a newly baptized child is clothed in a white garment and adults are clothed in white robes after baptism at the Easter Vigil.)

Amice (pronounced "A-miss"): A rectangular white linen cloth, stamped or embroidered with a cross. The priest puts it over his head and wears it around his neck and shoulders. This is the first vestment the priest puts on.

Chasuble: This is the most important Mass vestment. It is large and full and made of rich cloth. It comes in various liturgical colours. (Note: Colours used in vestments and altar coverings indicate special times in the liturgical year of the Church. Green is used in Ordinary Time. Red is for feasts of martyrs or the Holy Spirit. Purple is used in penitential times, such as Lent. White is for joyful occasions, including Christmas, Easter and some saints' days.)

Cincture: A long cord that the priest ties around his waist to hold the alb in place.

Stole: A long, narrow piece of cloth. Priests today wear the stole around the neck and hanging straight down in the front. (The stole is the chief priestly vestment. The chasuble sets the presider apart, but all priests who are concelebrating the Mass must wear a stole.)

Faith Facts

What Jesus Taught

Here are just a few of the teachings of Jesus from the gospels. Share these teachings with the children and talk about them together. Then have each child choose one to remember and write it out and illustrate it on a piece of paper. (You may have to help with the writing.) They can place these in their prayer corner at home.

1. Do not be angry with your brother or sister.
2. Keep your promises.
3. If anyone hits you, don't hit back.
4. Don't worry. God will take care of you.
5. If someone is hungry, share food with them.
6. Give to everyone who asks for your help.
7. If someone wants to borrow something from you, be generous.
8. Love your enemies and pray for those who hurt you.

All of these are important, but here is Jesus' greatest rule:

9. Love one another as I have loved you.

—all adapted from the Gospels

Faith Facts

Why We Use Wine at Mass

At the time of Jesus, grapes were harvested in the fall, and Passover (the time of the Last Supper) is in the spring. Without refrigeration, grapes (and grape juice) do not keep very well. Within a few days after the harvest, grapes begin to ferment or break down. In the first century, the only way to preserve fruit was to extract the juice and let it ferment under somewhat controlled conditions (make wine) or to dry the grapes (raisins).

They made wine from a number of different fruits, but the wine of the grape, the "fruit of the vine," was the one used at Passover. Since this was spring, and the Passover liturgy called for all participants to drink four cups of wine, grape juice preserved by fermentation (wine) was most certainly used. The directions for celebrating the Passover called for the cups of wine to be diluted with water because the wine was very strong. Also, the clay vessels they kept the wine in were somewhat porous; the wine tended to become thick over time as moisture escaped.

Faith Facts

More About Prayer

1. There are many beautiful prayers in our Catholic tradition that have a place in our class prayer. Among them are the Hail Mary, Our Father, Glory to God, Act of Contrition, and the prayers of the Mass. When you use formal prayers with children, try to keep them lively and not routine.
   - Divide prayers into parts and have the children read them in chorus.
   - "Chant" formal prayers instead of simply reciting them. (Chanting is done by choosing one note or tone and saying/singing the prayer that way.)
   - Invite the children to close their eyes and recall the presence of God before you say a formal prayer. (Never use formal prayers to silence children.)

2. Designate one place in your teaching area as the prayer space. This can be a desk, a small stand, or a portable table. Gather in this space for your class prayer.

3. Use prayers from the Mass and other liturgical rites. (The liturgy is under-taught, so use prayers and rituals from it often to reinforce their meaning.)

4. Share celebrations of the Word by carrying the Bible in procession to your prayer space and proclaiming the Scripture passage used in your lesson. Invite the children to take turns proclaiming the Word. Encourage them to speak slowly and clearly.

5. Use background music from time to time to create an atmosphere of calm and quiet.

Notes

Notes